Tokenomics Unleashed

Tokenomics Unleashed

FTT And The Future Of Finance

Rayan Musk

ROSE PUBLISHING

CONTENTS

INDEX 1

INTRODUCTION 3

Chapter 1 6

Chapter 2 22

Chapter 3 38

Chapter 4 53

Chapter 5 65

Chapter 6 78

Chapter 7 90

Chapter 8 104

Chapter 9 120

INDEX

1. **Introduction**
   1. Definition of Tokenomics
   2. Importance of Tokenomics in the Financial Landscape
   3. Rise of FTT (Finance Tokenized Token) as a Game-Changer

Chapter 1 Foundations of Tokenomics

1. Understanding Blockchain Technology
   1. Overview of Blockchain
   2. Smart Contracts and their Role

B. Tokenomics Fundamentals

1. Tokens vs. Traditional Assets
2. Token Creation and Distribution

Chapter 2 The Genesis of FTT

1. Introduction to FTT
2. Historical Development and Evolution
3. Key Features and Characteristics
   1. Speed and Efficiency
   2. Security and Transparency

Chapter 3 FTT in Action

1. Decentralized Finance (DeFi)
2. Tokenized Assets

3. Cross-Border Transactions
4. B. Real-world Examples of FTT Implementation

Chapter 4 Tokenomics Unleashed
4.1 Impact on Traditional Finance
4.2 Tokenomics and Economic Inclusion
4.3 Potential Disruption to Existing Financial Models

Chapter 5 Regulatory Landscape
5.1 Current Regulatory Environment for FTT
5.2 Challenges and Opportunities
5.3 Future Regulatory Trends

Chapter 6 Risks and Security Concerns
6.1 Security Challenges in Tokenomics
6.2 Fraud and Hacking Risks
6.3 Mitigation Strategies and Best Practices

Chapter 7 FTT and the Global Economy
7.1 FTT as a Catalyst for Economic Growth
7.2 International Adoption and Collaboration
7.3 Implications for Developing Economies

Chapter 8 Future Trends and Innovations
8.1 Evolving Landscape of Tokenomics
8.2 Integration with Emerging Technologies (AI, IoT, etc.)
8.3 Predictions for the Next Decade

Chapter 9 Challenges and Opportunities for Investors
9.1 Investment Strategies in FTT
9.2 Potential Returns and Risks
9.3 Diversification in a Tokenized Economy

INTRODUCTION

The financial technology have advanced to previously unheard-of levels in the fast-paced digital era. In the middle of all the developments, Fungible Token Technology (FTT) has become a major force that will reshape the financial industry going forward. "Tokenomics Unleashed: FTT and the Future of Finance," a book, aims to disentangle the complex web of FTT and investigate its potential to revolutionize the financial sector.

1. **How Tokenomics Started**
   The voyage starts with an examination of the term tokenomics, which is a combination of the words "token" and "economics." The economic framework that controls the creation, allocation, and application of tokens in a blockchain network is known as tokenomics. We hope to clarify the fundamental ideas and provide insight into how these tokens function as the foundation of decentralized economies as we explore the nuances of tokenomics.
2. **FTT: An Extensive Exploration of Fungible Token Innovation**
   Fungible Token Technology, a paradigm that has fundamentally changed how we view and engage with digital assets, is at the center of our investigation. It is essential to comprehend the fundamentals of fungibility as well as the special characteristics that distinguish FTT from other token kinds. We will explore the technological nuances that make FTT a powerful force in the decentralized financial space as we set out on this trip.
3. **Foundations of Blockchain Technology: The FTT Canvas**
   In order to understand FTT, one must first understand blockchain, the underlying technology. The fundamental ideas of blockchain technology are explained in the third portion of this introduction, along with how FTT uses its decentralized design to provide security, transparency, and immutability. Readers will have a deeper knowledge of blockchain basics and be better able to recognize the mutually beneficial link that exists between FTT and this innovative technology.

4. **FTT in Practice: Practical Uses**

   Every technology's real-world applications are its genuine test. We'll travel through a variety of industries in this section to see FTT in operation. FTT has impacted several industries, including gaming, entertainment, finance, and supply chains. It has brought efficiency, transparency, and new opportunities to these domains.

   Through insightful case studies, we will see firsthand how FTT is transforming conventional wisdom and promoting creativity.

5. **Tokenomics: Handling the Financial Environment of FTT**

   Tokenomics is an active, dynamic economic model rather than merely a theoretical idea. This section examines the token economy of FTT by examining the distribution, issuance, and valuation of tokens. The conversation will encompass the different types of token issuance, such as Security Token Offerings (STOs) and Initial Coin Offerings (ICOs). Understanding FTT's economic underpinnings will help readers understand the variables affecting token valuation and pricing dynamics.

6. **Opportunities and Challenges in the FTT Ecosystem**

   Every technical advancement has its share of difficulties. We address the challenges and roadblocks that FTT must overcome in order to become widely used in this section. We will explore the intricacies that require careful navigation, from security issues to regulatory considerations. At the same time, we will draw attention to the numerous advantages that result from conquering these obstacles, opening the door for a stronger and more resilient FTT environment.

7. **Upcoming Developments and Innovations**

The FTT journey is an investigation into the future of finance, not a conclusion to the present. This section looks through the crystal ball to reveal the predicted developments and trends that will influence how FTT develops. The financial technology environment is expected to experience significant transformation due to the incorporation of emerging technologies like artificial intelligence and the Internet of Things, as well as developments in technology integration. These changes will have a ripple effect on the whole financial industry.

Vlll. **How to Use It Practically: Engaging with FTT**

One of the main goals is to enable readers to actively engage with the FTT ecosystem. We give techniques, risk considerations, and insights for prospective investors in this area, which serves as a practical guide for investing in FTT. Additionally, we discuss the fundamentals of developing smart contracts and offer a roadmap for expanding the FTT infrastructure for those wishing to contribute to the creation of FTT-based apps.

lX. **The Social Impact of FTT and Ethical Issues**

FTT has societal effects and ethical ramifications in addition to its technological and financial aspects. We must critically assess FTT's social inclusion, ethical considerations, and environmental sustainability as it continues to influence the financial world.

This section encourages readers to consider the moral implications of FTT and calls for its responsible development and implementation in accordance with wider society ideals.

1. **Definition of Tokenomics**
2. **Importance of Tokenomics in the Financial Landscape**
3. **Rise of FTT (Finance Tokenized Token) as a Game-Changer**

Chapter 1

Foundations Of Tokenomics

The term "tokenomics," which combines the words "token" and "economics," refers to the intersection of economic theory and technology that shapes the structure of digital assets in blockchain environments. Tokenomics' guiding principles explore the nitty-gritty of how digital tokens function, move, and gain value in decentralized networks. It is critical for developers, politicians, and investors to comprehend the foundations of tokenomics as blockchain technology develops and becomes more widely used.

1. **Evolution of History:**
   The origins of tokenomics can be found in the launch of Bitcoin in 2009, which marked the arrival of blockchain technology. The goal of Bitcoin, which was designed as a decentralized money, was to create transparent and trustless financial transactions. But it was Ethereum's rise to prominence that really broadened the field of tokenomics.
   When Ethereum was first released in 2015, it introduced the idea of smart contracts, which made it possible to create decentralized apps (DApps) and issue different kinds of tokens. This signaled the transformation from a straightforward trade system to a more intricate one in which tokens might signify ownership, control protocols, and enable a wide range of interactions in decentralized ecosystems.
2. **Essential Elements of Tokenomics:**
1. **Use of Tokens:**
   Tokenomics is primarily concerned with the use that tokens have in their respective ecosystems. Comprehending the diverse functions of tokens is essential to appreciating their economic importance.
   Medium of Exchange: A lot of tokens are mainly used to facilitate trades between users inside the blockchain network. This is similar to how Bitcoin was originally intended to be used—as a peer-to-peer electronic cash system.

Access Rights: In a blockchain network, tokens frequently provide access to particular features or services. This can range from using a DApp's premium features to taking part in decentralized governance.

Governance: A significant change in the tokenomics scene has been the emergence of governance tokens. By enabling holders to take part in decision-making, these tokens enable a more decentralized and community-driven form of governance.

2. **Distribution and Supply of Tokens:**

   Evaluating the potential value and ecosystem impact of a token requires an understanding of the supply dynamics and distribution mechanisms.

   Fixed vs. Inflationary Supply: Tokens can be subject to inflationary models, in which new tokens are continuously introduced into circulation, or they can have a fixed supply, reflecting the scarcity principles of traditional commodities.

   Token Sales: Methods such as Initial Exchange Offerings (IEOs), Security Token Offerings (STOs), and Initial Coin Offerings (ICOs) are frequently used for the first distribution of tokens. By using these strategies, the project hopes to raise money and provide tokens to more people.

   Vesting: Tokenomics frequently includes vesting plans, which progressively release tokens over time for developers and early contributors in order to align incentives and prevent hasty sell-offs.

3. **Incentives and Token Economics:**

Tokenomics is the application of economic principles to the creation of incentive systems that promote desirable network behaviors.

Consensus Mechanisms: Tokenomics is greatly impacted by the consensus mechanism selected, be it Proof of Work (PoW), Proof of Stake (PoS), or variants such as Delegated Proof of Stake (DPoS). These systems have an impact on the incentives given to users for safeguarding the network and verifying transactions.

Staking: To take part in network activities and receive rewards, users must lock up a specific number of tokens. The blockchain network is becoming more decentralized and secure as a result of this process.

Tokenomics models may include mechanisms such as buybacks, in which the project uses earnings to repurchase and retire tokens, or burns, in which a percentage of tokens is permanently withdrawn from circulation. The goals of these procedures are to maximize token value and manage supply.

III. Obstacles and Things to Think About:

Notwithstanding the potential of tokenomics, a number of issues and concerns need to be resolved if it is to expand and be accepted over time.

1. **The Regulatory Environment**

   Globally, there are differences in the regulatory framework pertaining to token launches and cryptocurrencies. Governments and regulatory agencies are putting a lot of effort into creating frameworks that strike a balance between investor protection and innovation. Regulations that lack clarity can have a big impact on how token-based systems are developed and used.

2. **Scalability and Security:**

Blockchain networks have issues with scalability and security. Smart contract flaws and high-profile attacks underscore the importance of strong security protocols. Furthermore, scalability becomes essential for preserving transaction speed and cutting costs as blockchain networks expand.

Interoperability, or

C.One of the ongoing challenges is ensuring that several blockchain networks and their corresponding tokens work together. Achieving smooth communication and value transfer across many ecosystems is crucial for the wider adoption of decentralized technology, as the number of blockchain initiatives keeps growing.

D. Accessibility and User Experience:

User experience and accessibility are critical for widespread adoption. Enhancements in wallet technology, user interfaces, and instructional materials can help conventional users better understand the intricacies of blockchain technology.

IV. Prospective Patterns and Advancements:

The future of tokenomics is being shaped by a number of trends and innovations that are occurring in the blockchain and cryptocurrency world.

1. **Autonomous organizations that are decentralized (DAOs):**
   A major advancement in decentralized governance is represented by DAOs. These are blockchain-based organizations with smart contract governance that allow for decentralized decision-making without the need for a central authority. Because DAOs increase community involvement in governance, it is anticipated that they will have a significant impact on how tokenomics develops in the future.
2. **Solutions for Cross-Chains:**In order to tackle the issue of interoperability, cross-chain solutions are becoming more and more popular. By facilitating smooth communication and value transfer between various blockchain networks, these solutions hope to foster a more interconnected and cooperative ecosystem.
3. **Tokens for Privacy:**Tokens with a privacy focus are starting to appear in response to worries about data confidentiality and privacy. These tokens enable consumers improved privacy features through the use of cutting-edge cryptographic techniques, an important factor in an increasingly digital environment.
4. **Tokens for Sustainability:**Some blockchain projects are looking into integrating sustainability tokens since environmental sustainability is becoming more and more important. By providing incentives for eco-friendly behavior within

blockchain networks, these tokens hope to support the larger objectives of sustainability.

1. **Understanding Blockchain Technology**

Blockchain technology is a decentralized and safe method of handling digital transactions. It is frequently cited as one of the most revolutionary inventions of the twenty-first century. Fundamentally, a blockchain is a distributed ledger that makes information recording visible and impervious to tampering possible. Gaining an understanding of the complexities of blockchain technology is crucial to appreciating its many uses, ranging from supply chain management to cryptocurrency and beyond.

1. **Basics of Blockchain Technology:**
1. **Decentralization:**
   Blockchain technology's fundamental feature is its decentralized structure. A blockchain, in contrast to conventional centralized systems, is a distributed network of nodes, each of which keeps a copy of the whole ledger. By preventing any one party from controlling the network as a whole, decentralization promotes transparency and lowers the possibility of manipulation.
2. **Transactions and Blocks:**
   A blockchain is made up of a series of blocks, each of which has a list of transactions. "Mining" or "validation," depending on the network's consensus method, is the process by which these transactions are compiled and added to the blockchain. The information is arranged chronologically thanks to the block structure, creating an unchangeable chain.
3. **Cryptography:**

To ensure the confidentiality and integrity of transactions, Blockchain significantly depends on cryptographic methods. A hash, which is a special identification for every block, is produced by a sophisticated mathematical method. The blockchain is tamper-evident because altering any data in a block would need recalculating the hash for that block as well as all subsequent blocks.

II. Mechanisms of Consensus:
Consensus techniques are essential for maintaining network participants' agreement on the blockchain's current state. Distinct blockchain networks have diverse consensus processes, each possessing advantages and disadvantages.

1. **Proof of Work (PoW):**
   PoW is the most well-known consensus method. It challenges network users, or miners, to figure out challenging arithmetic problems. The block is validated and added to the blockchain by the first miner to solve the puzzle. PoW is quite

safe, but it uses a lot of processing power, which raises questions about how energy-efficient it is.

2. **Proof of Stake (PoS):**
As a PoW substitute, PoS chooses the validator for a new block by considering the quantity of cryptocurrency that each participant is ready to "stake" as security. Although this approach is more energy-efficient than proof-of-work, centralization may present difficulties because individuals with more stakes have greater sway.

3. **Delegated Proof of Stake (DPoS):**
The democratic aspect of DPoS is introduced by enabling token holders to select a small number of delegates who will verify transactions and add new blocks. The goal of this system is to bring together the advantages of decentralization with quicker transaction times.

4. **Proof of Authority (PoA):**

Rather than computing power or stake, validators in PoA are chosen based on their identity or reputation. When using a private or permissioned blockchain, where users are recognized entities, this consensus method is frequently employed.

III. Smart Contracts:

These self-executing contracts have their terms encoded directly into the code. When certain circumstances are satisfied, these contracts automatically come into effect and enforce the terms that were agreed upon. The creator of smart contracts, Ethereum, opened the door to a new era of decentralized applications (DApps) by giving programmers a platform to design and implement programmable contracts on the blockchain.

1. **Decentralized Applications (DApps):**
Dapps use smart contracts to carry out transactions and impose regulations, and they make use of blockchain technology to develop applications that function without a central authority. These applications are used in many different industries, such as supply chain, gaming, and banking.

2. **Decentralized Autonomous Organizations (DAOs):**

DAOs are blockchain-based entities that are controlled by smart contracts. They facilitate decentralized decision-making by giving members the opportunity to cast votes on ideas pertaining to the operations of the organization. DAOs signify a change in governance toward community-driven policies.

IV. Blockchain Technology Use Cases:

Blockchain technology brings efficiency, transparency, and security to a wide range of sectors. Among the noteworthy use cases are:

1. **Cryptocurrencies:**
   The emergence of cryptocurrencies and blockchain technology go hand in hand. The original cryptocurrency, Bitcoin, offered a decentralized, censorship-resistant kind of virtual money. Ethereum, Ripple, and Litecoin are a few of the later cryptocurrencies that have each added special features and applications.
2. **Supply Chain Management:**
   By logging each transaction and the movement of commodities on an immutable ledger, blockchain improves supply networks' transparency and traceability. This guarantees genuineness and aids in locating and resolving problems like contamination or fraud.
3. **Healthcare:**
   By offering a safe and compatible platform for healthcare data, blockchain technology can safeguard the exchange and storage of medical records. Patients will be able to manage their health information more effectively, and medical professionals will have access to current, accurate records.
4. **Finance and Banking:**
   A variety of financial services, like as lending, borrowing, and decentralized exchanges, are produced via Decentralized Finance (DeFi) platforms using blockchain technology. By operating without conventional middlemen, these platforms increase consumers' financial inclusion.
5. **Identity Management:**

By offering a safe and unchangeable record of a person's identity, blockchain technology provides a defense against identity theft and fraud. Users can choose the personal information they disclose and have more control over it.

V. Obstacles and Things to Think About:

1. **Scalability:**
   Scalability is a crucial issue as blockchain networks expand. Certain blockchains may have a limited transaction throughput, which could cause delays and increased fees during periods of strong usage.
2. **Interoperability:**
   Efficient communication and value transfer are hampered by incompatibilities throughout blockchain networks. There is continuous work being done to create interoperability standards and protocols.
3. **Regulatory ambiguity:**
   Users and businesses are facing ambiguity as the regulatory environment surrounding cryptocurrencies and blockchain technology changes. Regulations must be clear in order to promote innovation while maintaining security and protection for consumers.
4. **Energy Consumption:**

The significant energy consumption of Proof of Work consensus algorithms, such those used in Bitcoin, has drawn criticism. There is a continuous debate regarding the environmental impact of blockchain technology, which has led to the investigation of more energy-efficient consensus techniques.

1. **Overview of Blockchain**

The need for safe and decentralized digital transactions gave rise to blockchain technology, which has become a ground-breaking invention with broad applications in a variety of sectors. Fundamentally, a blockchain is a distributed ledger that uses a network of dispersed nodes to enable the transparent and unchangeable recording of data. This synopsis delves into the core ideas, essential elements, and possible uses of blockchain technology.

1. **Basic Ideas:**
1. **Dispersal:**
   The idea of decentralization lies at the core of blockchain technology. A blockchain runs on a peer-to-peer network as opposed to conventional centralized systems, which are governed and controlled by a single authority. As a result of maintaining an identical copy of the ledger on each node in the network, transparency is promoted and the possibility of manipulation or a single point of failure is reduced.
2. **Transactions and Blocks:**
   A blockchain's structure is centered on blocks, each of which has a list of transactions. After being validated, these transactions are added to the chain in a sequential and chronological manner by being bundled into blocks. The integrity of the complete transaction history is guaranteed by the linking of blocks using cryptographic hashes.
3. **Encryption:**

Blockchain uses cryptographic methods to protect transactional data. Every block in the chain is connected to the one before it by a hash, which is a distinct identification produced using a challenging mathematical method. This hash is essential to preserving the blockchain's immutability because any modification to a block would necessitate recalculating the hash for that block as well as all following blocks, rendering tampering very impossible.

II. **Important Elements:**

1. **Mechanisms of Consensus:**
   Consensus mechanisms are methods that guarantee consensus on the ledger's current state among nodes in a blockchain network. There are several consensus

methods available, each with advantages and disadvantages.

Proof of Work (PoW):

To validate transactions and produce new blocks, users, referred to as miners, must solve challenging mathematical puzzles. PoW uses a lot of energy yet is quite safe.

By selecting validators according to the quantity of cryptocurrency they own and are prepared to "stake" as collateral, Proof of Stake (PoS) operates. When it comes to energy efficiency, PoS outperforms PoW. By enabling token holders to select a small number of delegates to validate transactions, Delegated Proof of Stake (DPoS) combines decentralization with quicker transaction times.

2. **Intelligent Contracts:**

Self-executing contracts with terms encoded in code are known as smart contracts. When particular requirements are satisfied, they automatically carry out and enforce predetermined regulations. Decentralized applications (DApps) have been made possible by Ethereum, a leader in smart contract technology that offers developers a platform to design and implement these programmable contracts on the blockchain.

III. Prospective Uses:

1. **Digital Money:**

The emergence of cryptocurrency and blockchain technology are closely related. The notion of a digital money that is both censorship-resistant and decentralized was originally presented by Bitcoin, the pioneer cryptocurrency. Later cryptocurrencies, like Ethereum, have made it possible to create programmable and decentralized financial apps, expanding the use cases beyond simple transactions.

2. **Management of the Supply Chain:**

Supply chain management could undergo a change thanks to blockchain's capacity to provide traceability and openness. An unchangeable ledger records each transaction or movement of commodities, lowering fraud, guaranteeing authenticity, and improving accountability all the way up the supply chain.

3. **Medical Services:**

By protecting the exchange and storage of medical records, blockchain can help solve problems in the healthcare industry. Better care coordination results from patients having more control over their health information and healthcare providers having access to accurate and current records.

4. **Banking and Finance:**

Blockchain technology is used by Decentralized Finance (DeFi) systems to provide a variety of financial services, such as decentralized exchanges, lending, and borrowing. DeFi lessens dependency on centralized financial institutions and

improves financial inclusion by functioning without the use of conventional middlemen.
5. **Handling Identity:**

Blockchain offers an identity management system that is safe and impervious to manipulation. Users are in better control of the personal data they provide, sharing it only with those who require it. By doing this, the chance of fraud and identity theft can be greatly decreased.

IV. Obstacles and Things to Think About:

1. **Capability to Scale:**

Scalability becomes an issue as blockchain networks expand. Certain blockchains may have a limited transaction throughput, which could cause delays and increased fees during periods of strong usage.

Interoperability, or

B. Interoperability issues between several blockchain networks make it difficult to move currency and communicate easily. For a blockchain ecosystem to become increasingly interconnected, standards and procedures for interoperability must be established.

C. **Uncertainty in Regulations:**

Users and businesses are faced with uncertainty as the regulatory environment surrounding cryptocurrencies and blockchain technology changes. Regulations must be clear in order to promote innovation and guarantee the safety and security of consumers.

2. **Smart Contracts and their Role**

A ground-breaking feature of blockchain technology are smart contracts, which offer automated, self-executing contracts that have the ability to optimize a wide range of business operations. When certain requirements are satisfied, these blockchain-integrated digital contracts allow for the transparent and trustless implementation of predetermined rules. Gaining an understanding of smart contracts' function is crucial to appreciating its influence on decentralized systems as well as the larger commercial and technological landscape.

1. **Getting to Know Smart Contracts:**
1. **Code That Runs on Itself:**

   In essence, smart contracts are just strings of code that specify the parameters of a contract. They are contained within the blockchain, which guarantees their enforcement and execution devoid of middlemen. After it is deployed, a smart contract will automatically carry out its preprogrammed commands when certain criteria, or triggers, are satisfied.

2. **Transparency and Decentralization:**

Decentralized networks, such as Ethereum, Binance Smart Chain, or other platforms that allow for programmable functionality, are the setting in which smart contracts function. Because it is decentralized, there is less chance of manipulation and greater transparency because no one party can influence how the contract is carried out.

II. **Important Smart Contract Elements:**

1. **Logic and Code:**
A smart contract's code, which comprises the reasoning driving the arrangement, is its fundamental component. This code is created in programming languages like Solidity for Ethereum, which are especially intended for creating smart contracts. The logic lays forth the guidelines, requirements, and activities that the smart contract will carry out.

2. **Integration of Blockchain:**

The consensus mechanism of the underlying blockchain facilitates the execution of smart contracts, which are deployed on blockchain networks. The smart contract is safe against fraudulent operations because of the decentralized and tamper-resistant structure of the blockchain, which guarantees the contract's integrity.

III. **Smart Contracts' Function:**

1. **Process Automation:**
Process automation is one of smart contracts' main functions. Conventional contracts frequently call for manual verification, term fulfillment, and enforcement. By automatically carrying out operations when predefined circumstances are satisfied, smart contracts simplify these procedures by eliminating the need for middlemen and manual interventions.

2. **DeFi (Decentralized Finance):**
In the rapidly developing field of decentralized finance (DeFi), smart contracts are essential. They make it possible to create financial products without the use of conventional middlemen like banks, including lending, borrowing, and trading. DeFi platforms provide customers more control over their assets by automating complicated financial operations using smart contracts.

3. **Initial Coin Offerings (ICOs) and Tokenization:**
Tokenizing assets—representing ownership or rights in a digital format—is made easier by smart contracts. Smart contracts streamline the fundraising process for Initial Coin Offerings (ICOs), removing the need for a centralized authority and enabling companies to create tokens and distribute them to investors.

4. **Management of the Supply Chain:**
   Smart contracts improve traceability and transparency in supply chain management. They can automate the process of confirming the legitimacy of a product, start payments after a delivery is completed, and enforce quality control regulations. In addition to streamlining procedures, this lowers the possibility of fraud in the supply chain.
5. **Autonomous organizations that are decentralized (DAOs):**

The foundation of decentralized autonomous organizations (DAOs) is made up of smart contracts. Members of these code-governed entities cast tokens to vote on proposals. By implementing decisions in accordance with the results of the voting, smart contracts establish an automatic and transparent governance framework.

IV. Benefits and Difficulties:

1. **Benefits:**
   Efficiency: By automating procedures, smart contracts minimize the need for human interaction and streamline business operations.
   Transparency: All parties concerned can examine and confirm the conditions of the smart contract thanks to the decentralized and transparent nature of blockchain technology.
   Trustlessness: Participants can engage in agreements using smart contracts without depending on confidence in a central authority because they operate in a trustless environment.
   Cost reductions: Smart contracts can result in significant cost reductions by automating procedures and removing middlemen.
2. **Difficulties:**

Security Risks: Smart contract code weaknesses can be exploited, even though blockchain technology is inherently secure. Ensuring strong security protocols is essential.
Irreversibility: After they are implemented, smart contracts cannot have their terms altered. This could be a drawback if mistakes or unanticipated events occur.
Complexity: Creating and evaluating smart contracts can be difficult, requiring knowledge of blockchain security and development.

B. Tokenomics Fundamentals

The core of decentralized ecosystems is tokenomics, a portmanteau of "token" and "economics," which offers the financial framework for the production, transfer, and use of digital tokens inside blockchain networks. This complex area integrates ideas from game theory, cryptography, and conventional economics to create an environment that is both sustainable and rewarding for players.

We will examine the main ideas, difficulties, and wider ramifications of this changing economic paradigm in our examination of tokenomics foundations.

1. **The Core of Tokenomics: Token Utility**
1. **Exchange Medium:**
In the context of their individual blockchain networks, tokens frequently serve as a medium of trade. This function is best demonstrated by Bitcoin, the original cryptocurrency that allows peer-to-peer transactions without the use of middlemen. Some tokens, such as stablecoins, tie their value to conventional fiat money in an effort to keep it constant.
2. **Permission to Enter:**
In a decentralized economy, tokens often grant holders access rights to particular features or services. Holding governance tokens, for example, may allow users to vote on protocol changes in decentralized finance (DeFi) platforms, promoting a democratic governance paradigm.
3. **Oversight:**

A key component of decentralized decision-making is governance tokens. By voting on proposals or modifications to network parameters, holders of these tokens are able to take part in governance procedures. Participatory models like this one improve community involvement and decentralization.

II. **Token Distribution and Supply: Access and Scarcity Dynamics**

1. **Inflationary versus Fixed Supply:**
Tokens might follow a fixed supply paradigm, which would be similar to traditional commodities' concepts of scarcity. One such example is Bitcoin, which has a 21 million unit supply cap. Conversely, some tokens use inflationary strategies, which gradually add new tokens to the market.
2. **Initial Public Offerings and Token Sales:**
Events such as Initial Exchange Offerings (IEOs), Security Token Offerings (STOs), and Initial Coin Offerings (ICOs) are frequently the starting points for token distribution. These fundraising techniques disperse tokens to a larger audience in addition to providing funding for project development.
3. **Lockup and Vesting Periods:**

Vesting schedules are a prominent component of tokenomics, which aims to match incentives and deter quick sell-offs. These timelines specify how team members and early contributors would receive tokens gradually over time, encouraging sustained participation.

III. **Incentives and Token Economics: Creating a Self-Sustaining Ecosystem**

1. **Mechanisms of Consensus:**
   The selection of consensus methods has a significant impact on tokenomics. Participants are paid for validating transactions and safeguarding the network in accordance with Proof of Work (PoW), Proof of Stake (PoS), and Delegated Proof of Stake (DPoS) models. The consequences of each mechanism for energy efficiency, decentralization, and security are distinct.
2. **Rewards and Staking:**
   Staking is a mechanism by which users can earn rewards for contributing to network operations by locking up a specific number of tokens. Token holders are encouraged to actively participate in the network while also improving security through this process.
3. **Buybacks and Burns of Tokens:**

Tokenomics models can include processes such as buybacks, in which projects use earnings to repurchase and retire tokens, or burns, in which part of the tokens are permanently withdrawn from circulation. These tactics seek to increase value and regulate the supply of tokens.

IV. Obstacles and Things to Think About: Getting on with the Road Ahead

1. **Uncertainty in Regulations:**
   The global regulatory environment surrounding token offers and cryptocurrencies is still evolving. For participants to feel safe, encourage innovation, and guarantee compliance, regulatory frameworks must be clear.
2. **Dangers to Security:**
   Token functionality relies heavily on smart contracts, which potentially have flaws that can be taken advantage of. Thorough testing, regular audits, and continuous security measures are essential for reducing threats and safeguarding participants.
3. **Capability to Scale:**
   Scalability becomes important to take into account as blockchain networks grow. For wider adoption, it is crucial to make sure that the infrastructure can manage higher transaction volumes without sacrificing efficiency.
4. **Cooperativeness:**

It is necessary to handle the difficulty of ensuring that various blockchain networks and their coins are interoperable. The wider integration of decentralized technology requires smooth communication and value transfer across various ecosystems.

V. Prospective Patterns and Consequences: Handling the Changing Environment

1. **DeFi (Decentralized Finance):**
   Traditional financial services have changed due to the rapid expansion of decentralized finance. Tokenomics-powered DeFi systems increase financial inclusion by providing a variety of financial services without the need for conventional middlemen.
2. **NFTs, or non-fungible tokens:**
   In the world of digital assets, non-fungible tokens have become more and more popular as a means of proving ownership or authenticity for one-of-a-kind objects, digital artwork, and collectibles. The scarcity and value of these NFTs are determined in part by tokenomics.
3. **Autonomous organizations that are decentralized (DAOs):**

Token holders and smart contract-governed entities, or DAOs, represent the future of decentralized governance. Tokenomics makes DAO decision-making procedures easier and increases community involvement.

1. **Tokens vs. Traditional Assets**
   There are two different ways to express and possess values: tokens and traditional assets. For millennia, traditional assets have been the cornerstone of investment, having their roots in established financial systems. On the other hand, tokens provide a new paradigm for digital ownership and value transfer, particularly when considered in the context of blockchain technology and cryptocurrencies. The main distinctions between tokens and conventional assets are explored in this comparison.
   Conventional Resources:
   Conventional assets comprise a wide range of both material and immaterial possessions. These consist of fiat currencies, stocks, bonds, property, and commodities.
   Traditional asset ownership and transfers usually depend on centralized middlemen like banks, brokers, and clearinghouses. Ownership is documented in centralized systems, and transactions are governed by regulatory control.
   Traditional assets are characterized by their physical or legal representation. For example, a land deed reflects real estate ownership, and a stock certificate indicates ownership of a share of a firm.
   Conventional assets frequently entail convoluted procedures, documentation, and middlemen, which increases transaction costs and settlement timeframes.
   Geographic restrictions also apply to traditional assets, and cross-border transactions encounter delays and regulatory complications. Traditional assets are frequently inaccessible, which restricts participation to specific demographic groups and impedes global inclusivity.
   Insignias:

In the context of blockchain technology and cryptocurrencies in particular, tokens stand for a digital form of value and ownership. They use smart contracts to encode and carry out predetermined rules on decentralized networks like Ethereum and Binance Smart Chain. Token ownership is documented on an unchangeable, transparent blockchain ledger.

Tokens, in contrast to traditional assets, can stand for a wide range of assets, such as ownership of digital assets like non-fungible tokens (NFTs), cryptocurrencies, or utility within a platform. The simplicity with which tokens can be created and transferred enhances transaction efficiency by eliminating the need for middlemen and lowering related expenses.

Private cryptographic keys are frequently linked to token ownership, offering a safe and anonymous way to store assets. Peer-to-peer transactions are made possible by this decentralization, which promotes a trustless environment free from the need for centralized authorities.

Tokens also provide greater diversity and accessibility. Token-based ecosystems allow users from all over the world to join, removing conventional obstacles related to geography and demographics. Decentralized finance (DeFi) services, where users can lend, borrow, and trade digital assets without middlemen, have grown in popularity as a result of this feature.

2. **Token Creation and Distribution**

A crucial component of the digital economy is the creation and distribution of tokens, especially in relation to blockchain technology and cryptocurrencies. This procedure entails creating digital tokens and then distributing them to users in a decentralized network. Comprehending the processes involved in token generation and distribution is essential to understanding how different blockchain ecosystems operate.

Token Generation:

Smart contracts, self-executing bits of code that specify the characteristics and regulations of the token, are frequently used to expedite the production of tokens.

The entire token supply, the process for creating new tokens, and any particular features attached to the token are a few examples of these regulations. Ethereum, Binance Smart Chain, and other platforms with smart contract capability are the most widely used for token production.

Tokens can be used for a variety of things, such as facilitating governance in a decentralized organization or serving as a cryptocurrency (such as Bitcoin). The blockchain can represent a variety of assets, rights, or utilities thanks to the token creation's versatility.

Distribution of Tokens:

Tokens must be given to network participants after they are produced. Token distribution can be accomplished using a variety of techniques, each with unique ramifications for the project and its community:

Initial Coin Offerings (ICOs): ICOs are a means of raising money for projects in which tokens are sold to investors. Contributions are accepted in the form of well-known cryptocurrencies, and participants get a share of the newly issued tokens in accordance to their contributions.

Airdrops: A free token distribution to current cryptocurrency holders is known as an airdrop. This technique is frequently applied to raise awareness, reward devoted users, or start a community from scratch.

Token Burns and Buybacks: Token burns are projects that purposefully destroy a portion of the token supply in order to lower it overall. In order to retire tokens from the market and repurchase them using project revenues, buybacks also help regulate supply.

Mining and Staking: Participants in proof-of-work (PoW) and proof-of-stake (PoS) consensus methods stake tokens or provide processing power to validate transactions. In exchange, they are rewarded with freshly created tokens.

The project's financial model, decentralization, and community involvement are all impacted by the distribution method selection.

Chapter 2

The Genesis Of FTT

One important tool for policy in the areas of public finance and economic governance is the Financial Transaction Tax (FTT). The goal of this tax, also referred to as a Tobin tax, is to impose a tiny charge on a variety of financial transactions, including currency exchanges and stock trading. The FTT's origins can be linked to historical developments, economic theories, and the requirement for financial industry regulations. This paper investigates the development of the Financial Transaction Tax, looking at its theoretical underpinnings, historical background, and current implementation-related discussions.

Philosophical Underpinnings:

The concept of taxing financial transactions originated in the 1970s and is frequently linked to American economist and Nobel winner James Tobin. Tobin first brought up the idea of a currency transaction tax in his Princeton University Janeway Lectures in 1972. Tobin's main goals were to stabilize global financial markets and dissuade short-term, speculative currency trading. He maintained that while a tiny tax on foreign exchange transactions would have little effect on long-term commerce and investment, it could discourage speculative activity.

Tobin's suggestion sprang from his apprehension regarding the potentially disruptive consequences of speculative trading, particularly inside the foreign exchange markets. He thought that these kinds of actions were a contributing factor to both economic and currency volatility. The idea behind the so-called Tobin tax was to create a turbulence in the financial system that would discourage short-term speculative trading.

Historical Background:

Although Tobin's concept attracted scholarly interest, in the 1970s and 1980s it did not acquire much support in the policy arena. But in the wake of the 2008 global financial crisis, there was a resurgence of interest in the concept of taxing financial transactions. The financial system's vulnerabilities were made evident by the crisis, which prompted officials to review the regulatory framework and consider ways to keep similar incidents from happening in the future.

The scale of high-frequency and speculative trading, which many thought had contributed to the volatility of financial markets, was made clear by the financial crisis. As a result, a number of interested parties, including scholars, legislators, and advocacy organizations, started reexamining Tobin's proposal for a financial transaction tax as a means of reducing excessive speculation and raising money for the general welfare.

Initiatives in Europe:

In Europe, the demand for a FTT grew, and a number of nations expressed interest in putting one into place. A proposal for a common FTT to be adopted in 11 member states of the European Union was released by the European Commission in 2011. The principal aims were to produce income for EU member states, dissuade speculative trading, and establish a more stable financial system.

The implementation of a unified FTT was hampered by the disparate financial markets and regulatory environments among EU member states. The intended single FTT had not been completely implemented as of the knowledge cutoff in January 2022 because to disagreements among member states over the nature and scope of the tax. These disagreements caused delays and discussions.

Global Views and Difficulties:

Although the concept of a FTT was well received in certain areas, it was met with resistance and suspicion in others. Opponents contend that this kind of tax might reduce trading profits, impair market liquidity, and even force financial operations to countries lacking a financial transaction tax (FTT). An FTT's efficacy would depend on its broad international adoption due to the global structure of financial markets and the interdependence of economies.

In the absence of an international agreement, certain nations have adopted their own FTTs. In 2012, for instance, France imposed a 0.2% tax on the acquisition of shares in French companies with a market capitalization of more than €1 billion as part of the financial transaction tax. In a similar vein, Italy imposed a tax of that kind in 2013. But the reach of these national initiatives has been narrow, and they haven't offered a complete answer to the problems brought on by the world's financial markets.

Discussions and Obstacles:

There have been continuous discussions on the FTT's implementation, with both supporters and opponents putting forth different points of contention. An FTT, according to its supporters, can be used as a tool to combat wealth disparity, generate income, and maintain the stability of the financial system. They argue that a well-crafted FTT can lessen market volatility, deter short-term speculative trading, and produce a sizable amount of cash for public uses.

Opponents, however, express worries about the possible harm that a FTT could do to capital development, market liquidity, and economic expansion. They contend that the tax may cause financial activity to relocate to countries without a financial treaty, creating a dispersed and ineffective global financial system. Unintended consequences, such decreased market liquidity and higher trading costs, which could negatively impact investors and market participants, are another point of contention raised by critics.

To make matters more difficult, creating and executing a successful FTT is a complex process. Careful thought must be given to defining the taxable transactions, deciding on the proper tax rate, and resolving problems pertaining to cross-border transactions. For policymakers, finding a balance between accomplishing the intended policy goals and minimizing any unfavorable effects is extremely difficult.

Current Advancements:

There had been ongoing global discussions and arguments about the FTT as of the January 2022 knowledge cutoff. In order to create and execute a unified FTT, member states of the European Union continued to present difficulties. Concurrently, certain nations, such as the US, looked into the potential of enacting a national financial transaction tax.

The concept of a First-Term Referendum (FTT) garnered significant interest in the United States, especially amid the 2020 Democratic primary contests. A financial transaction tax was suggested by a few candidates as part of a larger plan to combat economic inequality and finance social programs. The direction of FTT talks in the US, however, would be greatly influenced by the results of the presidential election and ensuing political events.

1. **Introduction to FTT**

    In order to control the financial markets and raise money for the government, one policy measure that has gained popularity recently is the Financial Transaction Tax (FTT). The FTT, often called a Tobin tax after economist and Nobel laureate James Tobin, is intended to impose a little charge on a range of financial operations, including currency exchanges, stock trades, and bond transactions. This essay offers a thorough overview of the Financial Transaction Tax, examining its goals, theoretical underpinnings, historical background, and the international environment surrounding its implementation.

    Origins & Background History:

    The idea of a currency transaction tax was first put up by James Tobin in the early 1970s, which is when the FTT first emerged. Tobin proposed that a tiny tax on foreign exchange transactions could discourage short-term speculative trading and help maintain the stability of global financial markets in his 1972 Janeway Lectures at Princeton University. Tobin's main concern regarding the destabilizing implications of speculative activities, especially in the foreign exchange markets, was the driving force behind his suggestion.

    Tobin's proposal, meanwhile, did not take off in the field of policy right away.

A distinct economic environment, centered on financial market liberalization and deregulation, prevailed in the 1970s and 1980s. Not until the 2008 global financial crisis did the FTT resurface as a major policy issue.

The vulnerabilities and risks associated with excessive speculation and high-frequency trading were exposed by the financial crisis of 2008. Economists and policymakers started reexamining Tobin's suggestion as a possible means of reducing speculative activity and promoting stability in the financial markets. The crisis led to a reevaluation of the structure and operation of the financial system as well as a resurgence of interest in regulatory actions.

Philosophical Underpinnings:

James Tobin, who won the 1981 Nobel Prize in Economic Sciences for his contributions to the discipline, is largely responsible for the theoretical underpinnings of the FTT. Tobin's suggestion to impose a currency transaction tax was predicated on the notion of creating market friction to deter speculative short-term trading. The main idea was to charge transactions slightly in order to deter people from engaging in such activities.

Tobin contended that the levy would discourage speculative trading while having little effect on long-term investments and legitimate trade. For Tobin, the FTT might stabilize exchange rates and avert the destabilizing consequences of financial speculation on the actual economy by preventing excessive currency speculation and short-term capital flows.

Although Tobin's idea was first centered on foreign exchange transactions, the FTT's concept has since expanded to include a wider variety of financial markets and products. The fundamental idea is still the same: impose a tiny tax on financial transactions to encourage stability, deter excessive speculation, and raise money for public uses.

Goals for the FTT:

Given its complex effects on financial markets and the overall economy, the Financial Transaction Tax is intended to accomplish a number of interconnected goals. The main goals consist of:

Financial Market Stability: Encouraging the financial markets to remain stable is one of the FTT's main objectives. The tax is intended to curtail high-frequency trading and short-term speculative trading, which in turn helps to avert financial crises by slowing down market volatility.

Keeping Abnormal Speculation at Bay: The FTT is designed to keep excessive speculating in the financial markets at bay. Speculative actions can lead to asset bubbles and market distortions, particularly if they are motivated by short-term financial gain. By adding a fee to each transaction, the tax aims to reduce the appeal of such activities.

Revenue Generation: Creating money for the government is one of the FTT's main goals. The tax, even at a low rate, can amass significant money because of the amount of financial activities that take place on a global scale. The money raised could go toward supporting infrastructure improvements, public services, or other social and economic concerns.

Reducing Income disparity: By taxing financial transactions, which frequently provide high-frequency traders and financial institutions with large income, proponents of the FTT contend that their legislation can help reduce income disparity. The tax's proceeds might be used to fund initiatives that advance social justice and economic equality.

Resolving Externalities: The FTT is thought to be a means of resolving externalities pertaining to financial transactions. The wider economy may be impacted by high-frequency trading and speculative activity, which could result in systemic hazards and market imbalances. Through a transaction tax, the FTT seeks to internalize some of these externalities in order to improve the efficiency and stability of the financial system.

Global Environment and Application: The Financial Transaction Tax's adoption has generated controversy and debate on a global scale. In certain places, the concept has been well received, while in others, it has encountered opposition and suspicion. The worldwide reach of financial markets and the interdependence of economies provide obstacles to the successful execution of the Financial Treaty.

European Initiatives: The European Union (EU) made a noteworthy attempt to put the FTT into effect. A unified FTT was suggested by the European Commission in 2011 and was to be implemented in eleven EU member states. A variety of financial instruments, such as stocks, bonds, and derivatives, would be subject to the proposed tax.

The aim was to produce income for EU member states, dissuade speculative trading, and establish a more stable financial system.

Nonetheless, there were many obstacles in the way of the EU's adoption of a unified FTT. Diverse financial markets and regulatory environments across the member states resulted in debates on the tax's scope and design. The talks were made more difficult by concerns about things like the possible effect on market liquidity and the danger of financial activity moving to countries without a FTT. The intended unified FTT had not been fully implemented as of the January 2022 knowledge cutoff, and talks among EU member states had not ended.

National Initiatives: Some nations have taken the lead in implementing their own versions of the FTT in the lack of a worldwide agreement. Remarkably, in 2012, France imposed a 0.2% tax on the acquisition of shares in French companies with a market capitalization of more than €1 billion as part of a financial transaction tax. In a similar vein, Italy imposed a tax of that kind in 2013. Although these national programs were a start in the right direction toward putting the FTT into effect, their reach was constrained in comparison to the more expansive plan of a complete, global transaction tax.

The implementation of the Fair Trade Treaty (FTT) has been greeted by a multitude of opinions and obstacles on a worldwide scale. The tax's supporters contend that it is an essential instrument for correcting market imperfections, fostering stability, and raising funds for public uses. They argue that a more equitable and long-lasting financial system can be achieved through the FTT.

However, detractors express worries about the FTT's possible unfavorable effects. One of the main arguments against the tax is that it might cause trading costs to rise, market liquidity to decline, and financial activity to perhaps relocate to countries without a financial transaction tax (FTT). Due to the worldwide nature of financial markets, if a FTT is not implemented consistently throughout the major financial hubs, its efficacy may be jeopardized.

Discussions and Difficulties: The discussions surrounding the Financial Transaction Tax bring to light the difficulties and complications involved in putting it into practice. Among the main issues of disagreement are:

Effect on Market Liquidity: According to critics, the FTT may result in less market liquidity, which would make it more challenging for buyers and sellers to complete transactions. Increased trading expenses and broader bid-ask spreads could follow from this, especially for institutional investors.

Financial Activity Migration: There are worries that if the FTT is implemented in one jurisdiction, financial activity may move to another where there is no such tax.

A global financial system that is fragmented and has distinct laws and taxation in different places could be the outcome of this.

unforeseen Consequences: The possible unforeseen effects of the FTT must be carefully considered by policymakers. For instance, a tax that is not well thought out may cause market distortions or open doors for some types of transactions to avoid paying taxes.

Choosing the Tax Rate: Selecting the right tax rate for the FTT is a difficult issue. A rate that is too low might not meet the targeted revenue and regulatory goals, while a rate that is too high could negatively impact market activity.

Defining Taxable Transactions: A key component of creating a functional FTT is determining the extent of taxable transactions. To make sure the tax is both broad and targeted, it is important to carefully assess which financial products and transactions should be subject to it.

Current Developments: Until the knowledge deadline in January 2022, there were ongoing global talks and arguments on the FTT. In order to create and execute a unified FTT, member states of the European Union continued to present difficulties. Concurrently, certain nations, such as the US, looked into the potential of enacting a national financial transaction tax.

The concept of a First-Term Referendum (FTT) garnered significant interest in the United States, especially amid the 2020 Democratic primary contests. A financial transaction tax was suggested by a few candidates as part of a larger plan to combat economic inequality and finance social programs. The direction of FTT talks in the US, however, would be greatly influenced by the results of the presidential election and ensuing political events.

2. **Historical Development and Evolution**

From its theoretical beginnings to current discussions, the Financial Transaction Tax's (FTT) historical growth and evolution reflect shifting financial markets, crises in the banking industry, and the continuous search for efficient regulatory solutions. This story takes place across a number of decades, looking at significant turning points, conceptual foundations, and practical attempts to put the FTT into practice.

Philosophical Underpinnings:

The idea of a currency transaction tax was first put up by Nobel laureate economist James Tobin in the early 1970s, which is where the FTT originated.

Tobin was motivated by his worries that speculative trading, especially in foreign exchange markets, could have a disruptive effect. In order to deter short-term speculative trading and calm global financial markets, he proposed a tiny tax on foreign exchange transactions, which he presented at Princeton University's Janeway Lectures in 1972.

The underlying assumption of Tobin's proposal was that the tax would discourage speculative activity without materially hindering legitimate commerce or long-term investment. Tobin sought to alleviate the volatility brought on by speculative trading and short-term capital movements by creating friction in the financial markets.

Early Acceptance and Ineffectiveness:

Tobin's concept, while appealing in theory, did not immediately take off in the field of policy. Global financial liberalization and deregulation took place in the 1970s and 1980s, creating a climate that was less accommodating to policies thought to impede market efficiency. The idea of a transaction tax had trouble becoming widely accepted by financial organizations and legislators during this time.

Because of this, Tobin's idea was mostly limited to academic discourse, and there were few attempts to enact this kind of tax in the actual world. The FTT and other regulatory measures were subordinated to market efficiency and freedom in the then-dominant economic ideology.

Resurgence following the Financial Crisis of 2008:

When the world financial crisis hit in 2008, everything changed drastically. The financial system's weaknesses were made clear by the crisis, which also highlighted the dangers of excessive risk-taking, speculative trading, and a lack of adequate regulatory control. Following the crisis, researchers, economists, and advocacy organizations reexamined the regulatory frameworks that were in place and looked at ways to keep similar incidents from happening again.

The financial crisis brought Tobin's concept back into the public eye and made the FTT a more attractive option for addressing systemic concerns and making money. The desire to reduce speculative activity and support the stability of financial markets gave rise to the idea of taxing financial transactions.

Initiatives in Europe:

The European Union's (EU) attempt to impose a common tax was one of the major turning points in the FTT's historical evolution. A comprehensive FTT was suggested by the European Commission in 2011 and was to be implemented in eleven EU member states. The proposed tax was intended to be applied to a variety of financial items, such as derivatives, stocks, and bonds, with the main goals being to increase market stability and provide money to member states.

But there were several obstacles in the way of the EU's single FTT. Diverse financial markets and regulatory environments across the member states resulted in debates on the tax's scope and design.

The negotiations became more contentious due to issues including the possible impact on market liquidity and worries about financial operations moving to jurisdictions without a FTT.The intended single FTT had not been fully implemented as of the January 2022 knowledge cutoff, and discussions among EU member states continued. The European endeavor demonstrated how challenging it may be to come to an agreement on a complicated regulatory policy that calls for coordinated action across many economies.

Domestic Applications:

Some nations choose to execute the FTT on a national level in the lack of a unified international strategy. In this sense, France led the way by enacting a financial transaction tax in 2012. The French FTT levied a 0.2% tax on the acquisition of shares in French corporations with a market capitalization more than €1 billion.

In 2013, Italy unveiled its own version of the FTT, following suit. These national initiatives were attempts to solve particular issues in the financial markets in which they were implemented. They did, however, also draw attention to the difficulties in implementing a thorough and well-coordinated strategy for taxing financial activities globally.

Global Views and Difficulties:

There are still differing opinions on the FTT throughout the world, with supporters highlighting its possible advantages and opponents raising worries about how it may affect market dynamics. Proponents contend that the FTT can increase revenue for public uses, reduce excessive speculation, and stabilize the financial system.

However, detractors point up a number of difficulties and possible negative

effects connected to the FTT:

Market Liquidity Fears: According to critics, the FTT may result in less market liquidity, which would make transactions more challenging for buyers and sellers. Increased trading expenses and broader bid-ask spreads could follow from this, especially for institutional investors.

Financial Activity Migration: There are worries that if the FTT is implemented in one jurisdiction, financial activity may move to another where there is no such tax. A global financial system that is fragmented and has distinct laws and taxation in different places could be the outcome of this.

unforeseen Consequences: The possible unforeseen effects of the FTT must be carefully considered by policymakers. For instance, a tax that is not well thought out may cause market distortions or open doors for some types of transactions to avoid paying taxes.

Choosing the Tax Rate: Selecting the right tax rate for the FTT is a difficult issue. It takes careful thought to strike the correct balance between meeting revenue and regulatory goals without placing an undue burden on market participants.

Defining Taxable Transactions: A key component of creating a functional FTT is determining the extent of taxable transactions. To make sure the tax is both broad and targeted, it is important to carefully assess which financial products and transactions should be subject to it.

Current Advancements:

There had been ongoing global discussions and arguments about the FTT as of the January 2022 knowledge cutoff. In order to create and execute a unified FTT, member states of the European Union continued to present difficulties. Concurrently, certain nations, such as the US, looked into the potential of enacting a national financial transaction tax.

The concept of a First-Term Referendum (FTT) garnered significant interest in the United States, especially amid the 2020 Democratic primary contests. A financial transaction tax was suggested by a few candidates as part of a larger plan to combat economic inequality and finance social programs. The direction of FTT talks in the US, however, would be greatly influenced by the results of the presidential election and ensuing political events.

3. **Key Features and Characteristics**

A tool for policy that has attracted attention is the Financial Transaction Tax (FTT), which has the ability to control the financial markets and provide funds for public uses. The design and impact of the FTT have been shaped by a few essential aspects and qualities that have developed from the evolving conversations surrounding it. These core ideas are examined in this essay, which also offers insights into the nature of the FTT and its effects on economies and financial markets.

1. **Transaction Coverage:** The FTT's ability to handle a wide range of financial transactions is one of its key characteristics. Usually, the tax is applied to a number of different kinds of transactions, such as currency exchanges, bond sales, and stock trades, among others. A key component of the FTT's design is the scope of taxable transactions, and legislators must precisely specify which financial instruments and activities are subject to the tax. This characteristic has a direct impact on how well the FTT accomplishes its goals.
2. **Tax Rate:** The effect of the FTT on financial markets and revenue collection is significantly influenced by the tax rate. It takes careful balance to determine the right tax rate. An excessively high rate may deter proper market activity, decrease liquidity, and even force financial activity to areas where there is no Financial Treaty. Conversely, a tax rate that is too low could not meet the tax's revenue and regulatory goals. The best tax rate for the FTT must be carefully considered by policymakers while taking economic factors and market dynamics into account.
3. **Revenue Generation:** Creating money for the general public's use is one of the FTT's main goals. The amount and frequency of taxable transactions determine how much money the tax can raise. Supporters contend that because of the size of the world's financial markets, the FTT has the potential to generate large amounts of money, even at a relatively low rate. The money made might go toward building infrastructure, paying for public services, or tackling social and economic problems. The tax's real revenue impact is contingent upon several factors, including its design, implementation, and the reactions of market participants.
4. **Market Stability and Speculation:** The FTT's possible influence on speculative activity and market stability is another important aspect of the law. Proponents contend that by discouraging short-term speculative trading, the tax can lower market volatility and stop disruptive movements. In order to reduce the risk of asset bubbles and market distortions, the FTT seeks to establish a more stable financial environment by discouraging excessive speculation. Critics, however, voice worries that the fee may reduce market liquidity and may have unforeseen effects on trading behavior, which can exacerbate market imbalances.
5. **International collaboration:** To ensure that the FTT is implemented effectively, international collaboration is required due to the global character of financial markets. Achieving agreement on the tax's structure and implementation, in addition to resolving worries about the possible relocation of financial activity to areas without a financial transaction tax, is a difficult task for policymakers. The absence of a unified strategy may cause regional variations in tax rates and structures, which could cause fragmentation in the world's financial markets. To guarantee the FTT's efficacy and avoid regulatory arbitrage, international cooperation is necessary.

6. **Administrative Mechanisms:** Strong administrative procedures for compliance, enforcement, and collection are necessary for the FTT's implementation. For the purpose of tracking and taxing eligible transactions, policymakers must set up effective and transparent procedures.

   This entails dealing with issues pertaining to international transactions, liaising with financial institutions, and putting in place measures to stop tax evasion. To maximize anticipated results and assess the efficacy of the FTT, the administrative infrastructure is essential.

7. **Effect on Market Participants:** One important factor to take into account is how the FTT will affect different market players, such as traders, investors, and financial institutions. The impact on various market participants may vary depending on their trading techniques, transaction volume, and overall business structures. The tax's effect on transaction volumes and liquidity, for instance, may result in increased costs for institutional investors who engage in high-frequency trading. In order to prevent undue disruption of financial activity or unforeseen consequences, policymakers must evaluate the possible effects on market players.

8. **Examining Exemptions:** When drafting the FTT, legislators frequently think about whether specific transactions or market participants need to be spared from paying the tax. Certain kinds of transactions or financial instruments may be exempted in order to prevent impeding essential market operations or endeavors that further wider economic goals. To avoid any unexpected distortions in market behavior, it is necessary to carefully analyze the scope and grounds for exemptions.

9. **Possibility of Behavioral Shifts:** The use of the FTT could cause players in the market to adopt different behaviors. In reaction to the levy, traders and investors may change their tactics or the frequency of their trades. Policymakers must comprehend these possible behavioral shifts in order to predict how the tax will affect market dynamics, liquidity, and overall efficiency. It also emphasizes how crucial it is to keep an eye on market reactions and modify the FTT's parameters as needed.

10. **Addressing disparity and Social Objectives:** Proponents of the Financial Transaction Tax (FTT) frequently point out that by taxing financial transactions—which provide high-frequency traders and financial institutions with a sizable revenue stream—they may help solve the problem of income disparity. The tax's proceeds could be used to fund social programs, efforts to combat poverty, or other projects that advance economic equality. To make sure the FTT works well toward societal goals, policymakers must match its design with more general social and economic aims.

11. **Changing Regulatory Environment:** The FTT functions inside the larger framework of financial industry regulation. Its inception and development take

place against the backdrop of shifting regulatory environments influenced by financial crises, global economic conditions, and financial technological breakthroughs.

To maintain consistency in the entire approach to financial market governance, policymakers must take into account how the FTT complements and aligns with current regulatory frameworks.

1. **Speed and Efficiency**

When implementing the Financial Transaction Tax (FTT), speed and efficiency are important factors that affect how well the tax works to achieve its revenue and regulatory goals. Policymakers must strike a compromise between the necessity of guaranteeing effective market operations and the expediency of implementation when they develop and execute the FTT. The importance of speed and efficiency in FTT implementation is explored in this essay, along with its consequences for financial markets, regulatory frameworks, and the overall state of the economy.

1. **Quick Implementation for Market Impact:** The financial markets may be directly impacted by how quickly the FTT is put into place. Market disruptions and protracted uncertainty can be avoided with prompt and decisive implementation. Speculative activity could arise as a result of prolonged uncertainty or delays surrounding the tax's implementation, as market players try to adjust to possible shifts in trading tactics. In order to minimize negative market reactions and promote a seamless transition to the new regulatory environment, timely implementation is essential.
2. **Finding a Balance Between Efficiency and Regulatory Complexity:** Implementing FTT efficiently requires finding a balance between the necessity for a streamlined framework and regulatory complexity. The FTT must be created by policymakers to be effectively administered while avoiding needless complications that can impede market activity. The FTT is made more efficient overall by its simple tax structures, effective administrative procedures, and transparent and unambiguous regulations. Simplified procedures improve adherence and lessen the workload for market players, enabling a more efficient and long-lasting tax system.
3. **Technology and High-Frequency Trading:** One important consideration is the speed of financial transactions, especially in the high-frequency trading (HFT) era. High-frequency traders place and execute a lot of orders very quickly —often in a matter of microseconds. It is necessary to take into consideration the technological features of contemporary financial markets when implementing the FTT.

It is imperative for policymakers to guarantee that the tax can be effectively imposed on high-frequency transactions without resulting in any disturbances or unforeseen outcomes. In order to record and execute transactions in real-time, which reflects the pace at which financial markets function, technology integration in FTT systems is essential.

4. **Cross-Border Transactions and Global Coordination:** Taking into account cross-border transactions and global coordination is crucial to the effectiveness of FTT implementation. Global financial markets exist, and international cooperation is necessary for the FTT to be effective. To avoid regulatory arbitrage, policymakers must handle issues pertaining to cross-border transactions, harmonize tax laws across countries, and guarantee that taxes are imposed consistently. Inadequate coordination across various regions can result in inefficiencies, market distortions, and possible financial activity migration to countries with disparate tax regimes.

5. **Administrative Efficiency:** The administrative procedures designed to gather and enforce the FTT are essential to its overall effectiveness. Market participants' compliance expenses are minimized and timely and transparent tax collection is guaranteed by an effective administrative system. Strong administrative systems that can manage the volume and complexity of financial transactions are something that policymakers must invest in. The FTT is successful in accomplishing its revenue and regulatory goals because of its efficient data processing, precise tracking of taxable events, and strong enforcement measures.

6. **Market Liquidity and Transaction Costs:** The effect that FTT has on market liquidity and transaction costs is directly related to how well it is implemented. In order to prevent unduly decreasing market liquidity, which can make it more difficult for buyers and sellers to transact, the tax rate and design must be carefully considered. Overly high transaction costs have the potential to discourage market participation or have unforeseen effects like wider bid-ask spreads. Maintaining a liquid and efficient market while balancing the FTT's revenue generation objectives is a difficult task that needs serious thought from policymakers.

7. **Flexibility in Implementation:** The FTT framework's ability to adjust to shifting economic dynamics and market conditions is another aspect of efficiency. It is recommended that policymakers incorporate mechanisms into the tax architecture that enable them to adapt to changing market conditions and technology improvements. A flexible strategy guarantees the FTT's continued applicability and efficacy over time, taking financial market changes into account without sacrificing its regulatory objectives.

8. **Evaluation of Unintended implications:** Policymakers must carefully evaluate any potential unintended implications of the FTT, even though efficiency and speed are crucial. Unintended disruptions could result from rapid

implementation without a full understanding of market dynamics and associated adverse effects. Policymakers must interact with market participants, carry out in-depth effect evaluations, and be ready to modify plans in response to results. This iterative process guarantees that the FTT accomplishes its goals without causing unanticipated distortions or adverse effects.

2. Security and Transparency

To maintain the Financial Transaction Tax's (FTT) efficacy, integrity, and market players' acceptance, a careful balance between security and transparency must be struck during implementation. Transparency promotes confidence, compliance, and a clear understanding of how the tax works, while security measures protect the FTT system against fraud, manipulation, and unauthorized actions. The relationship between security and transparency in the context of FTT implementation is examined in this essay.

Security Procedures:

Data security and privacy: Gathering and handling private financial information is a necessary part of implementing the FTT. Data security and privacy must be given top priority in security measures in order to adhere to ethical and legal requirements. Strict access controls, secure data storage procedures, and strong encryption techniques are necessary to stop illegal access and safeguard the privacy of financial data.

Authentication and Authorization: Strong authentication and authorization procedures are essential to the security of FTT installation. Preventing fraud and manipulation requires making sure that only authorized individuals or institutions may access and edit FTT-related data. The FTT system's overall security is enhanced by permission-based access management, secure login processes, and multi-factor authentication.

Cybersecurity Protocols: The FTT system needs to have strong cybersecurity protocols because cyber threats are becoming more sophisticated. This includes proactive steps to reduce potential cyber threats, real-time monitoring for suspicious activity, and routine vulnerability assessments. Cybersecurity frameworks must to be flexible and dynamic in order to accommodate changing financial risks.

Fraud Prevention and Detection: Security protocols must to be created with the intention of stopping and identifying fraudulent activity pertaining to FTT transactions.

Abnormality detection, pattern recognition, and real-time monitoring automated systems can assist in spotting anomalies and possible fraud cases. It is necessary to have quick reaction systems in place to handle and lessen security breaches.

Transaction Integrity: The viability of the tax depends critically on maintaining the integrity of FTT transactions. It should be ensured by security measures that transactions are accurately recorded and unchangeable. The decentralized and unchangeable ledger of blockchain technology has been investigated as a possible means of improving transaction integrity in the application of FTT.

Measures of Transparency:

Unambiguous Tax Laws: Transparency starts with unambiguous and easily understood tax laws. Market players must comprehend the FTT's application, the transactions that will be taxable, and the corresponding tax rates. Lack of clarity or complexity in the tax laws can result in misconceptions, noncompliance, and a diminished sense of confidence in the FTT system.

Public Communication: Establishing trust in the FTT requires open and honest communication with the general public and market players. It is imperative for policymakers to furnish transparent and prompt information regarding the tax's objectives, the implementation process, and any adjustments or modifications made to the FTT structure. A deeper comprehension of the tax and its effects is facilitated by frequent and easily available communication.

Reporting and Disclosure: Extensive reporting and disclosure systems contribute to increased transparency. In addition to ensuring accountability, regular reporting on FTT revenue collection, allocation, and utilization enables stakeholders to monitor the tax's effects. Practices of transparent disclosure help to build public trust in the FTT's efficacy and fairness.

Public Consultation: To obtain feedback from a range of stakeholders, policymakers should participate in public consultation procedures in the spirit of transparency. Getting input from investors, financial institutions, and the general public guarantees that different viewpoints are taken into account while designing and executing the FTT. The process of making decisions is made more inclusive and transparent when public engagement is encouraged.

Audit and Oversight: Clear oversight procedures, such as regulatory reviews and external audits, are essential to maintaining the FTT system's integrity.

Independent audits support the establishment of trust in the fairness of the tax system, help confirm conformity with tax legislation, and pinpoint possible areas for improvement. One factor that enhances the transparency of FTT operations is regulatory oversight.

Keeping Transparency and Security in Check:

For the FTT to be successful, a careful balance between security and transparency must be struck. Achieving this balance requires keeping openness to foster confidence among stakeholders while putting strong security measures in place to safeguard the integrity of the tax system.

Transparency shouldn't be compromised by security measures, and vice versa. For example, robust encryption safeguards confidential information, but it shouldn't impede the openness of reporting systems. Transparent communication should also avoid disclosing any information that would jeopardize the FTT system's security.

Furthermore, the continual enhancement of security and transparency measures is facilitated by the incorporation of stakeholder comments through transparent engagement processes. Policymakers may address new issues, adjust to changing financial environments, and improve the FTT's overall efficacy thanks to this iterative approach.

Chapter 3

FTT In Action

The notion of a Financial Transaction Tax (FTT) has gained traction as a regulatory instrument that may influence financial markets, deal with systemic problems, and produce income for the government. A wide range of experiences that are gaining traction as different jurisdictions investigate the application of FTTs offer important insights into the usefulness of this policy instrument. This thorough investigation examines the FTT in operation, evaluating its effects on income generation, financial markets, and international viewpoints on its application.

1. **Strategies for Implementing FTT:**

    1.1 Scope and Design: The goals and considerations unique to each jurisdiction are reflected in the scope and design of FTTs, which vary. The scope establishes the categories of financial transactions—stocks, bonds, derivatives, and high-frequency trading—that are liable to taxes. To accomplish the intended regulatory aims without unreasonably interfering with market activity, policymakers must carefully consider which financial products are subject to the tax.

    Important components of the FTT's design include tax rates, exemptions, and administrative procedures. Tax rates need to be balanced between preventing negative effects on market liquidity and producing significant income. To avoid unforeseen repercussions, specific transactions or market participants may be granted exemptions. The administrative framework—which includes procedures for enforcement, compliance, and collection—is essential to the FTT's successful execution.

    1.2 Tax Rates and Revenue Generation: A key factor in the implementation of FTT is the establishment of suitable tax rates. The difficulty is in adjusting rates to meet revenue targets without suppressing the market. While higher tax rates can deter excessive speculation, they also run the risk of reducing market liquidity and possibly pushing financial activity to countries without financial treaties. On the other hand, reduced tax rates might not bring in enough money to cover the demands for public support.

Generation of FTT income is dependent on the number and regularity of taxable transactions. Proponents contend that the size of the global financial markets may generate significant revenues for public uses even at very modest rates. It is imperative for policymakers to meticulously evaluate the revenue impact, taking into account the structure, enforcement, and reactions of market actors to the tax.

1.3 Market Impact and Behavioral Shifts: The deployment of a FTT invariably modifies the dynamics of the market and causes participants to alter their behavior. To lessen the impact of the levy, traders, investors, and financial institutions may modify their trading tactics, frequency of trades, or the kinds of instruments they use. Seeing these shifts in behavior offers important information into how flexible market players are and how resilient the financial system is to changes in regulation.

An important area of examination is the effect on trade volumes, transaction costs, and market liquidity. The effectiveness of price discovery and variations in bid-ask spreads are important markers of how market players handle the tax. If policymakers want to make sure that the FTT accomplishes its goals without creating unforeseen problems, they need to keep a careful eye on these market dynamics.

2. **Obstacles and Things to Take Into Account When Implementing FTT:**

   2.1 International collaboration: To ensure the successful implementation of the FTT, international collaboration is required due to the global character of financial markets. Achieving agreement on the tax's structure and implementation, in addition to resolving worries about the possible relocation of financial activity to areas without a financial transaction tax, is a difficult task for policymakers. The absence of a unified strategy may cause regional variations in tax rates and structures, which could cause fragmentation in the world's financial markets.

   The goal of international coordination initiatives, like the G20 negotiations, is to reduce the possibility of regulatory arbitrage and harmonize FTT rules. To create a unified worldwide strategy for FTT deployment, policymakers must successfully negotiate the challenges of balancing a variety of economic interests and regulatory agendas.

   2.2 Unintended Repercussions and Market Distortions: The use of FTT may have unanticipated repercussions and cause market distortions. Inadvertently favoring specific market participants or causing trading methods to alter in a way that defeats the purpose of the tax are two outcomes of poorly planned taxes. In order to anticipate possible distortions in market behavior, policymakers must undertake comprehensive impact evaluations. They should also be ready to adjust the tax system in order to handle any unforeseen repercussions.

Resolving unforeseen consequences calls for a flexible and quick regulatory strategy. Frequent evaluations, stakeholder involvement, and feedback systems guarantee that the FTT stays in line with its intended objectives while reducing unfavorable side effects.

2.3 Flexibility in Adapting to Changing Financial Environments: Financial markets are ever-changing, constantly adapting to new developments in technology, changes in the economy, and modifications to regulations. For FTT frameworks to continue to work over time, they must show that they can adjust to these shifting environments. Changes in market structures, new trends in trading activities, and advancements in financial technology must all be taken into account by policymakers when determining how to implement the tax.

Using processes for regulatory revisions and modifications is part of an agile approach to FTT deployment. For policymakers looking to guarantee the tax's continued relevance, case studies and experiences from jurisdictions that have effectively modified their FTT frameworks to shifting financial environments provide insightful information.

3. **Effect on Allocation and Revenue Generation:**

    3.1 Revenue Outcomes: Measuring the real money brought in by FTTs that have been put into place gives a concrete indication of the tax's budgetary impact. A few examples of the variables that impact revenue results are the tax rate, the volume of taxable transactions, and the general state of the financial markets. The revenue statistics must be examined by policymakers in order to assess how well the FTT achieves its financial goals.

    Studies that compare the revenue outcomes of various jurisdictions provide valuable insights into the elements that lead to prosperous revenue production. From these experiences, policymakers may improve revenue outcomes, hone tax arrangements, and make sure that money raised are in line with social interests.

    3.2 distribution and Utilization: Important components of FTT implementation, apart from income creation, are the distribution and utilization of money. The allocation of FTT money to infrastructure projects, public services, and other approved uses must be done transparently by policymakers. Transparent reporting on the distribution and use of revenue promotes accountability and guarantees that the tax makes a significant contribution to achieving social objectives.

    Understanding the wider effect of the tax on public finances can be gained by examining how jurisdictions distribute and use the money they receive from the FTT. To improve the FTT's societal advantages and meet urgent social and economic needs, policymakers might take a cue from effective revenue allocation models.

4. **International Views and New Developments:**

4.1 Technological Innovations: An rising trend in the context of FTT implementation is the incorporation of technological innovations, including blockchain. The decentralized and unchangeable ledger of blockchain technology presents an opportunity to improve the efficacy and transparency of FTT systems. Blockchain can help FTT systems operate more effectively by guaranteeing the accuracy of transaction data and expediting the tax collecting process.

Examining how technological advancements are being adopted by FTT systems provides insight into how regulatory frameworks may develop in the future. In order to improve the operational effectiveness and security of FTT implementation, policymakers can evaluate the viability, advantages, and difficulties of implementing such technology.

4.2 worldwide Collaboration and Standardization: A commitment to harmonizing tax structures and coordinating regulatory measures is shown in the continuous pursuit of worldwide collaboration and standardization in FTT implementation. International initiatives to reduce the risk of regulatory arbitrage and advance fair competition in the world's financial markets include talks held inside the G20.

Examining the advancements and obstacles in global cooperation offers valuable perspectives on the future of standardized FTT frameworks. In order to improve their own strategies for implementing FTT and to be in line with larger international initiatives, policymakers should learn from these initiatives.

4.3 Environmental, Social, and Governance (ESG) Considerations: As the emphasis on sustainable and socially responsible investing grows, environmental, social, and governance (ESG) factors are becoming more and more important in the financial markets. Future developments in FTT implementation could involve matching regulatory actions with more general societal and environmental goals, as well as taking ESG factors into account when designing taxes.

Examining how FTTs integrate ESG standards and support sustainable finance offers insights into the changing regulatory priorities for the financial markets. These tendencies offer policymakers ideas on how to improve the social and environmental effects of FTTs.

1. **Decentralized Finance (DeFi)**

The old financial environment is undergoing a radical paradigm shift with the advent of Decentralized Finance, or DeFi. DeFi, which is based on the ideas of decentralized systems and blockchain technology, seeks to establish an accessible financial environment by doing away with middlemen and giving users more authority. This essay examines the fundamental ideas, important elements, difficulties, and potential consequences of the quickly developing field of decentralized finance.

1. **Fundamental Ideas of DeFi:**
   1.1 Decentralization: The decentralization idea is the foundation of DeFi. In contrast to conventional financial systems, which depend on centralized organizations like banks or middlemen, DeFi makes use of blockchain technology to build a peer-to-peer, trustless financial infrastructure. On the blockchain, self-executing code known as "smart contracts" automates financial transactions and does away with the need for middlemen.
   1.2 Smart Contracts: These are programmable contracts that, upon the fulfillment of certain circumstances, take automatic action. These contracts, which are based on blockchain systems like Ethereum, allow for the development of decentralized apps (DApps) that support a variety of financial activities, including as asset management, lending, borrowing, and trading. DeFi protocols are transparent and automated thanks to smart contracts.
   1.3 Tokenization: Tokenization is the process of turning physical assets like money, commodities, or real estate into digital tokens that may be stored on a blockchain. Due to their ease of trading, these tokens offer partial asset ownership and liquidity. DeFi uses tokenization to produce a wide variety of financial products that let consumers engage with assets in ways that aren't feasible in conventional finance.
2. **Essential Elements of DeFi:**
   2.1 Decentralized Exchanges (DEXs): The core of DeFi trading is comprised of decentralized exchanges. DEXs function without middlemen, in contrast to centralized exchanges, enabling users to trade straight from their wallets. Token swaps are made easy and trustworthy by the use of automated market makers (AMMs) driven by smart contracts on platforms such as Uniswap and SushiSwap.
   2.2 Lending and Borrowing Procedures: DeFi presents lending and borrowing procedures that function independently of conventional banking institutions. Users can borrow assets by collateralizing their holdings or lend their digital assets and earn interest using platforms such as Compound and Aave. These systems give customers more flexibility and efficiency by automating the loan and borrowing procedures through the use of smart contracts.
   2.3 Stablecoins: Stablecoins are digital currencies that provide stability in erratic cryptocurrency markets by being indexed to the value of conventional fiat money. Stablecoins such as DAI and USDC are essential to DeFi's lending, trading, and other financial operations. These reliable assets serve as a link between the traditional and decentralized financial domains.
   2.4 Decentralized Autonomous Organizations (DAOs): DAOs are organizations managed by the collective will of the community and regulated by smart contracts. DAOs frequently participate in governance, fund management, and protocol update decision-making in the context of DeFi. A decentralized

method of project governance is fostered by the voting power that participants possess, which is based on the quantity of tokens they own.
3. **Difficulties in DeFi**
   3.1 Security Issues: Smart contract vulnerabilities have been the main source of major security issues for DeFi. Hacks, exploits, and coding flaws can cause large financial losses. In order to maintain user confidence and avert potential systemic breakdowns, identifying and mitigating security threats is a top focus as the ecosystem changes.

   3.2 legal Uncertainty: As the legal environment for DeFi changes, different countries are having difficulty classifying and regulating these decentralized financial systems. Uncertainty brought forth by unclear legislation may restrict the uptake of DeFi while consumers, developers, and organizations work through legal and compliance issues.

   3.3 Scalability Problems: A large number of DeFi applications are hosted on blockchain networks, especially Ethereum, which has scalability issues. Exorbitant gas prices and network congestion might cause inefficiencies, impeding DeFi's scalability and widespread adoption. The goal of Ethereum 2.0 development and Layer 2 solutions is to solve these scalability problems.

   3.4 User Experience and Accessibility: DeFi's complicated user interface may discourage widespread adoption. A prerequisite for interacting with decentralized apps is frequently a certain level of technical knowledge, and entrance barriers may arise from the absence of user-friendly interfaces. Increasing DeFi's user base will need making the platform more accessible and designing UI that are easier to use.

4. **Prospective Consequences and Patterns:**

   4.1 Cross-Chain Integration: More blockchain network interoperability could be a part of DeFi's future. Cross-chain solutions enable assets to transfer effortlessly between different blockchains in an effort to expand user options and get around scalability constraints.

   4.2 Integration with Traditional Finance: As DeFi develops, more integration with traditional finance is probably in store. Collaboration between centralized and decentralized systems may be necessary for this to happen, enabling the smooth passage of funds and other resources between the two domains. The improvement of regulatory clarity may lead to an increase in institutional participation in DeFi.

   4.3 Evolution of Decentralized identification: Improving security and privacy in DeFi transactions is the goal of decentralized identification solutions. Decentralized identity systems might play a key role in user permission and authentication as the ecosystem develops, guaranteeing a private and safe banking experience.

   4.4 The Emergence of Decentralized Oracles: Decentralized oracles are essential for giving smart contracts access to outside data. The need for safe and decentralized

oracle solutions grows as more and more DeFi applications need real-time data. With the increasing sophistication of DeFi protocols, this tendency is anticipated to persist.

2. Tokenized Assets

Tokenized assets offer a digital form for real-world asset ownership and trading, marking a revolutionary convergence of blockchain technology and traditional banking. These digital representations have a number of advantages, such as improved transparency, fractional ownership, and better liquidity. They are frequently represented on blockchain platforms as tokens. The idea of tokenized assets is examined in this essay, along with its importance, underlying technology, and possible effects on the financial system.

1. **Being Aware of Tokenized Assets**

   Digital representations of physical assets, including as real estate and artwork, as well as conventional securities like stocks and bonds, are known as tokenized assets. On blockchain networks, these digital representations are produced by issuing tokens, each of which represents a fraction or share of the underlying asset. The procedure entails turning an asset's attributes and ownership rights into programmable smart contracts, which are subsequently tokenized and stored on a blockchain.

2. **Essential Elements of Assets Tokenized:**

   2.1 Smart Contracts: An essential part of the tokenization procedure are smart contracts. These self-executing contracts specify the terms and regulations that apply to the tokenized asset and are programmed on blockchain systems such as Ethereum. Aspects of ownership like as voting rights, dividend distributions, and other contractual duties related to traditional assets are automated by smart contracts.

   2.2 Blockchain Technology: The technology that underpins tokenized assets is blockchain, which offers a transparent and safe ledger. Because blockchain technology is decentralized, ownership records are dispersed over a network of nodes, which lowers the possibility of fraud and produces a transaction record that is difficult to tamper with. Tokenized assets are often created and traded on blockchain platforms like Ethereum, Binance Smart Chain, and others.

   2.3 Token Standards: The features and attributes of tokenized assets are defined by particular standards that they follow. ERC-20 is the most widely used standard for tokenized assets on the Ethereum blockchain for fungible tokens, whereas ERC-721 is the standard for non-fungible tokens (NFTs). By guaranteeing interoperability, these standards facilitate the trading of tokens among different platforms and the creation of decentralized apps (DApps) that communicate with these resources.

3. **Importance and Advantages of Assets That Are Tokenized:**

   3.1 Enhancement of Liquidity: Tokenization tackles the problem of liquidity that is typically connected to certain asset classes. Fractional ownership is made possible by tokenizing assets, allowing investors to purchase and sell smaller shares of valuable assets. Due to their enhanced divisibility, hitherto illiquid assets become more tradeable and accessible.

3.2 Fractional Ownership: The idea of fractional ownership is introduced by tokenized assets, which enable several investors to jointly own a portion of an asset. Once-exclusive markets are now open to a wider range of participants thanks to the democratization of ownership. In the real estate industry, where high property values frequently create obstacles to entry for private investors, fractional ownership has a particularly significant effect.

3.3 Global Accessibility: Tokenized assets' digital format makes them more globally accessible. Tokenized marketplaces allow global investors to participate without being restricted by location. This openness increases the pool of potential investors, draws a wide spectrum of players, and strengthens the bonds within the international financial system.

3.4 Automation and Efficiency: Several facets of ownership and transactions are automated via smart contracts that are integrated into tokenized assets. By cutting out middlemen and simplifying procedures like dividend distribution, compliance, and regulatory reporting, this automation improves operational efficiency. Because smart contracts are programmable, sophisticated financial instruments with predetermined terms and conditions can be created.

3.5 Enhanced Transparency: Transactions and ownership records are traceable and verifiable thanks to Blockchain's visible and immutable ledger. Investor confidence is increased as a result of the increased transparency, which lowers the possibility of fraud and other wrongdoing. Information on the blockchain that is available to the public makes the financial system more transparent and accountable.

4. **In Actual Use, Tokenized Assets:**

4.1 Real Estate: The real estate industry has made considerable use of tokenization. Tokenizing high-value assets like luxury homes or commercial real estate enables investors to buy and sell fractional ownership. Retail investors now have more ways to access real estate markets and diversify their holdings thanks to this.

4.2 Stocks and Equities: By tokenizing traditional stocks and equities, ownership in a corporation can be represented digitally. Fractional ownership is made possible via tokenized equities, allowing investors to purchase and sell smaller share units. This may result in more retail investors participating in the stock market and more liquidity.

4.3 Art and Collectibles: The market for art and collectibles is also covered by tokenization, which enables the ownership of priceless artworks or uncommon artifacts to be represented as tokens. This makes it possible for art aficionados to purchase and exchange fractional ownership of well-known works of art, democratizing access to the art world.

4.4 Venture Capital and Startups: Tokenization opens up a fresh perspective on financing venture capital and startups. Startups have the option to tokenize their ownership and provide investors with tokens in place of conventional equity funding. This strategy gives venture capital investments—which have historically been illiquid—liquidity and permits early-stage enterprises to have fractional ownership.

5. **Obstacles and Things to Think About:**

   5.1 Regulatory Environment: Tokenized asset regulations are subject to change and differ between states. To maintain compliance with current regulations and create an atmosphere that supports the expansion of tokenized asset markets, regulatory clarity is crucial. For regulators, finding a balance between investor protection and innovation continues to be a major challenge.

   5.2 Smart Contract dangers: Although smart contracts are efficient and offer automation, there are dangers associated with them if they are not sufficiently secured and audited.

   Smart contract code vulnerabilities may allow for financial losses and the possibility of exploitation. To keep people confident in tokenized assets, smart contracts must be reliable and secure.

   5.3 Educational Barriers: Many prospective investors might not be familiar with the idea of tokenized assets and blockchain technology. The broad adoption of tokenized assets depends on removing obstacles to education and creating user-friendly interfaces. To overcome these issues, raising awareness of blockchain technology and enhancing financial literacy are essential.

6. **Prospective Patterns and Conclusion:**

   6.1 Solutions for Cross-Chain Interoperability: Increased blockchain network interoperability could be a future feature of tokenized assets. Cross-chain solutions facilitate the smooth transfer of assets between several blockchains by addressing scalability concerns and offering users additional options. The ecosystem of tokenized assets may grow and liquidity may be improved by this interoperability.

   6.2 Integration with Traditional Finance: More integration with traditional finance is anticipated as the tokenized asset market develops. A smooth bridge between the two worlds can be built by cooperation between centralized and decentralized systems, facilitating the effective flow of assets and liquidity. As regulatory certainty increases, institutional interest in tokenized assets may also rise.

   6.3 Evolution of Security Tokens: As a means of proving ownership of physical goods and adhering to legal requirements, security tokens are probably going to become more widely used. These tokens serve as a link between traditional banking and the decentralized world by combining the advantages of tokenization with regulatory compliance.

3. Cross-Border Transactions

In the increasingly integrated global economy, cross-border transactions—the exchange of products, services, or financial instruments between individuals, enterprises, or financial institutions across national borders—play a crucial role. International trade, investment, and capital transfers depend on these interactions. This essay examines the intricacies, difficulties, and developments in cross-border transactions, illuminating the crucial factors to take into account when negotiating the complex international financial system.

1. **Cross-Border Transactions' Significance**

    1.1 International commerce: The exchange of goods and services between nations is made possible by cross-border transactions, which are the foundation of international commerce. Importing and exporting helps businesses expand their revenue streams, get access to new markets, and take advantage of their competitive advantages. The smooth movement of products across borders promotes international cooperation and economic prosperity.

    1.2 Capital Flows and Investment: Cross-border transactions encompass not only trade but also the transfer of capital and investment between countries. Investors diversify their portfolios and aid in the growth of emerging economies by looking for possibilities outside of their own markets. International investments stimulate economic growth, generate jobs, and stimulate innovation.

    1.3 Global Financial Integration: The process of integrating financial systems across borders is essential. Financial markets function as interdependent networks that provide users access to a wide range of currencies, investment opportunities, and financial instruments. The efficiency of capital allocation, price discovery, and liquidity are all improved by financial market integration.

2. **Crucial Elements of International Trade:**

    2.1 Foreign Exchange Markets: Acting as a market for the purchase and sale of various currencies, foreign exchange, or forex, markets are essential to cross-border operations. Currency exchange is a means by which participants—banks, businesses, and institutional investors—enable international trade and investment. The value of currencies in cross-border transactions is determined by exchange rates, which are impacted by a number of factors.

    2.2 International Payment Systems: The seamless completion of cross-border transactions depends on effective international payment systems. Financial institutions can securely communicate and settle with each other thanks to established methods like SWIFT (Society for Worldwide Interbank Financial Telecommunication). Blockchain and digital currency are two emerging technologies that are changing the game by providing quicker, more affordable options.

2.3 Trade Finance: The facilitation of cross-border trade transactions is greatly aided by trade finance. The risks involved in international trade are reduced by tools like letters of credit and trade finance programs offered by banks, which guarantee that importers receive the agreed-upon commodities and exporters are paid. These financial products give those taking part in cross-border transactions confidence.

3. **Obstacles in International Trade:**

    3.1 Currency Exchange Risk: One of the biggest obstacles to cross-border transactions is currency exchange rate changes. The cost of commodities, profitability, and general financial stability of companies involved in international trade can all be impacted by changes in exchange rates. To control and lessen the risk of currency exchange fluctuations, hedging techniques are used, such as forward contracts and options.

    3.2 Regulatory Compliance: One of the challenges in conducting cross-border transactions is navigating various and frequently complex regulatory regimes. Complexity is increased by adhering to various legal and regulatory frameworks, such as know your customer (KYC) and anti-money laundering (AML) regulations. Companies operating in different nations have restrictions that they need to be aware of and follow.

    3.3 Cross-Border Payment Friction: Inefficiencies, high transaction costs, and delays are frequently linked to conventional cross-border payment systems. Extended settlement timeframes may be the consequence of the multi-step process involving correspondent banks. The investigation of alternative payment methods and developing technologies has been prompted by the demand for increased speed, transparency, and cost-effectiveness.

    3.4 Cultural and Linguistic Disparities: When conducting cross-border business, cultural and linguistic variations can make communication difficult. Establishing rapport, settling disagreements, and negotiating conditions all depend on effective communication. Successful transactions and long-term collaborations are more likely when cultural differences are understood and navigated.

4. **Innovations and Advancements:**

    4.1 Blockchain Technology: With regard to cross-border transactions, blockchain technology has shown to be a revolutionary force. The technology of distributed ledgers provides efficiency, security, and transparency. Blockchain-based smart contracts automate and simplify a number of transactional processes, eliminating the need for middlemen. This technology has the power to completely change the current environment surrounding cross-border payments.

    4.2 Digital currencies and digital currencies issued by central banks (CBDCs):

Cross-border transactions are made possible by the emergence of digital currencies, such as cryptocurrencies and central bank digital currencies (CBDCs). Traditional payment methods can be replaced with faster and more affordable options using digital currency. Central banks may expedite settlement procedures and lessen reliance on middlemen by issuing CBDCs.

4.3 Real-Time Gross Settlement Systems: Real-time gross settlement (RTGS) systems improve the speed and effectiveness of cross-border payments by enabling the instantaneous settlement of transactions on a one-to-one basis. These systems offer almost rapid transaction confirmation while lowering counterparty risks. To modernize cross-border transactions, central banks and financial institutions are investigating and putting into practice RTGS technologies.

5. **Prospective Thoughts and Patterns:**

5.1 Interconnected Financial Ecosystems: More worldwide integration of financial ecosystems is necessary for cross-border transactions in the future. More interoperability of payment systems, simpler regulatory procedures, and improved connection amongst various financial markets are anticipated to contribute to a more efficient and smooth cross-border transaction environment.

5.2 Financial Inclusion: Increasing financial inclusion can be facilitated by developments in cross-border transactions. Through the use of digital technology, such as digital wallets and mobile banking, people in underserved areas can transact across borders and get access to international markets and financial services.

5.3 Sustainable Finance: Cross-border transactions are becoming more and more influenced by sustainability factors. Environmental, social, and governance (ESG) factors are being included by investors and businesses in their decision-making processes. Cross-border transactions are witnessing an increasing prevalence of sustainable finance methods such as responsible investment and green bonds.

B. Real-world Examples of FTT Implementation

Financial Transaction Taxes (FTTs) are a topic of discussion and attention on a worldwide scale as governments look for measures to reduce market volatility, raise money, and support financial stability. Although the idea of FTT is not new, different jurisdictions have different approaches, providing insightful real-world instances for analysis. This essay investigates multiple FTT implementation cases, looking at the reasons for, difficulties encountered, and results to gain understanding of the usefulness and consequences of this policy instrument.

1. **Sweden: A Pioneering Nation with Changing Rates**

    Sweden introduced the first version of a FTT in 1984, making it one of the early adopters. Over time, changes were made to the Swedish FTT, which was originally designed to target equity transactions. The nation broadened the tax's scope in 2012 to include derivatives and other financial instruments. After being relatively modest at first, the tax rates were raised in 1986 and then significantly modified in the years that followed.

Motivations: The main reason Sweden established the FTT was to increase government revenue. The tax also attempted to encourage more stable financial markets by discouraging excessive speculation.

Challenges: The possible movement of trading activity to countries without a free trade agreement (FTT) posed a difficulty for Sweden. The argument put out by critics was that this would cause market liquidity to decline and financial transactions to move to markets with lower or no transaction taxes.

Results: Although the FTT in Sweden brought in money for the government, there was disagreement on how it affected trading volumes and market behavior. Sweden's experience serves as a reminder of the necessity to carefully calibrate tax rates in order to balance the generation of revenue with any potential effects on market dynamics.

2. **France: Fair Trade Terms for Equity Deals**

2012 saw the implementation of a FTT in France, with a primary focus on equities transactions. The tax was levied on purchases of stock in businesses whose market value was more over one billion euros. The buyer was required to pay the 0.2% fixed rate. This strategy was directed at the equities market and was designed to produce income while preventing speculative short-term trading.

Motivations: France wanted to tax speculative and high-frequency trading in order to generate income through the FTT. Furthermore, the tax was thought to be a way to encourage longer-term, more reliable investing methods.

concerns: The fear that the FTT will result in less liquidity in the equity market was one of France's concerns. The tax, according to its detractors, would force trading activity to places where there is no tax, which could reduce the competitiveness of the French financial markets.

Results: The French FTT brought in money, but there was disagreement over how it affected trade volumes and market liquidity. There were changes made to the tax, and new exemptions were added. The French example highlights how crucial it is to thoroughly evaluate the scope and design of the FTT in order to accomplish the desired outcomes without unforeseen repercussions.

3. **FTT on High-frequency Trading in Italy**

2013 saw the introduction of a FTT in Italy aimed at high-frequency trading (HFT) operations. The levy was imposed on equity deals involving Italian businesses valued at more than 500 million euros. The tax applied to both buyers and sellers, with rates changing according on the kind of transaction (conventional trading was subject to a lesser rate, while HFT was subject to a higher one).

Motivations: By taxing HFT, Italy hoped to reduce speculative activity and raise money. The emphasis on differentiating between high-frequency trading and traditional trading was a subtle way to solve some issues related to frequent and quick transactions.

Difficulties: Like other countries, Italy has to deal with the possibility of trade activity moving to areas without a free trade agreement. There have also been discussions over the possible effects on market liquidity as well as the efficacy of targeting HFT.

Results: The difficulties in creating a tax that differentiates between various trading tactics were illustrated by the Italian experience with a FTT on HFT. Even though the tax brought in money, debates continued regarding how it affected market dynamics and if the goals it was meant to accomplish were being met.

4. **United Kingdom: Shares Stamp Duty**

    Stamp duty on shares is a long-standing FTT in the United Kingdom. The transfer of shares in UK corporations is subject to this tax, which was first imposed in 1694. The buyer is normally responsible for paying the current rate, which is 0.5% of the transaction value. The UK has continued to impose this stamp duty as a way to raise money over the years. Stamp duty on shares in the UK was primarily imposed for revenue-generating purposes. The tax is ingrained in the nation's financial structure and is seen as a dependable source of revenue for the government.

    Challenges: Since the tax raises the cost of share transactions, one issue the UK faces is the possible impact on market liquidity. The financial markets in the UK may become less competitive as a result, according to critics, particularly when compared to countries where transaction taxes are either nonexistent or very low.

    Results: The UK government has consistently received income from the stamp duty on shares. The effect on trade activity and market behavior, however, is still up for debate. The experience from the UK demonstrates the long-term viability of several FTT models as well as the necessity of striking a balance between revenue targets and possible impacts on market dynamics.

5. **Financial Transaction Tax Proposed for the European Union**

    EU has been investigating the potential for a unified FTT among its member states. Stocks, bonds, and derivatives are just a few examples of the financial items that would be subject to the proposed Financial Transaction Tax, also known as the EU FTT or FTT. The tax is intended to be imposed on transactions between big businesses and financial institutions.

    Motivations: The EU FTT aims to achieve a number of goals, including generating income and discouraging speculative trading. Furthermore, promoting a uniform approach to financial market regulation and preventing regulatory arbitrage are the goals of harmonizing taxes among EU member states.

    Challenges: Reaching an agreement among member states with disparate financial market systems and economic interests is one of the major obstacles facing the EU FTT. Prolonged negotiations have surrounded the proposed tax, and some member nations have voiced concerns about how it may affect their financial industries.

Results: The EU FTT is still in the proposal and negotiation stages as of this writing. The talks draw attention to how difficult it is to execute a harmonized FTT among a wide range of nations with different financial markets. The result will probably have an impact on how FTTs develop in the EU going forward.

6. **International Views: Difficulties and Issues**

Although the aforementioned instances shed light on how FTTs are implemented in particular legal contexts, the global view of FTTs is still complicated. A number of difficulties and factors come into play while doing a more thorough analysis of FTTs:

International Coordination: Because the world's financial markets are interconnected, international coordination is required for implementing financial technology transfer (FTT). It is crucial to coordinate strategies across nations due to worries about regulatory arbitrage and the possible relocation of trading activities to areas without FTTs.

Effect on Market Dynamics: It is important to take into account how FTTs will affect trading volumes, investor behavior, and market liquidity. Finding a balance between market efficiency and revenue generation necessitates a sophisticated comprehension of the ways in which FTTs impact various financial market areas.

Adaptability to Changing Environments: The financial markets are dynamic and always changing. It is imperative that FTT frameworks exhibit flexibility in response to evolving market dynamics, technological progress, and worldwide economic transformations. It can be essential to conduct recurring evaluations and modifications to guarantee the sustained efficacy of FTTs.

Unintended Consequences: Trading techniques may alter, the market may become more fragmented, or the makeup of market participants may change as a result of FTTs. In order to make well-informed modifications to FTT frameworks, policymakers need to closely monitor and evaluate these unexpected effects.

Competition vs. Harmonization: There is a conflict between the need for financial markets to be competitive and the harmonization of FTTs in order to prevent regulatory arbitrage. To make sure that FTTs support financial stability without compromising the competitiveness of particular jurisdictions, it is imperative to strike the correct balance.

Chapter 4

Tokenomics Unleashed

The term tokenomics, which is a combination of the words "token" and "economics," refers to the economic framework that controls the production, allocation, and application of tokens in a blockchain network. Tokenomics was first imagined as a way to facilitate decentralized digital currencies, but it has since developed into a complex field with applications in many different sectors of the economy. This paper investigates tokenomics' history, constituents, and effects, focusing on how it has influenced decentralized economies and creative business models.

1. **The Development of Tokenomics: From Decentralized Ecosystems to Cryptocurrencies**

    1.1 The Origins of Tokenomics: The 2009 launch of Bitcoin is considered the origin of tokenomics. A proof-of-work consensus mechanism was used by the first cryptocurrency, Bitcoin, to safeguard its network and compensate miners with newly minted bitcoins. This was the first instance of a decentralized framework's token-based reward mechanism. As additional blockchain startups with distinct native tokens and business models arose, the idea gained popularity.

    1.2 Ethereum and Smart Contracts: Tokenomics saw a paradigm shift in 2015 with the launch of Ethereum. Because Ethereum's smart contract feature made it possible to create tokens on its blockchain, the number of Initial Coin Offerings (ICOs) has increased. By distributing native tokens to early backers through these fundraising events, projects were able to build the groundwork for various token economies that go beyond straightforward money use cases.

    1.3 Interoperability and Token Standards: Token interoperability was aided by the creation of token standards, most notably ERC-20 and ERC-721 on the Ethereum network. For fungible tokens, ERC-20 tokens emerged as the industry standard, enabling easy interaction with a wide range of exchanges and decentralized apps (DApps). Concurrently, ERC-721 enabled the creation of unique digital assets such as digital art and collectibles by introducing non-fungible tokens (NFTs).

1.4 The Emergence of Decentralized Finance (DeFi): The emergence of Decentralized Finance (DeFi) marked a dramatic shift in tokenomics. Tokens are used by DeFi protocols to provide a variety of financial services, such as yield farming, decentralized exchanges, lending, and borrowing. With the rise in popularity of governance tokens like COMP (Compound) and MKR (Maker), users are now able to take part in the decision-making processes of decentralized protocols.

1.5 Beyond Finance: Real-World Asset Tokenization: Tokenizing physical assets allowed tokenomics to spread beyond the digital sphere. On blockchain networks, assets like property, artwork, and even stock in companies become programmable and convertible tokens. This movement profoundly changed traditional asset markets by providing greater liquidity, fractional ownership, and round-the-clock accessibility to the market.

2. **Tokenomics Components: An Overview of the Token Economy**

    2.1 Token Creation and Distribution: Token creation and distribution are the initial facet of tokenomics. Frequently, token production happens as a result of fundraising events, mining, or staking. Token distribution to early investors, users, community members, and founders is decided upon during the distribution phase. The process of creating and distributing tokens is essential to determining a project's initial economic framework.

    2.2 Use Cases and Utility: The value of tokens comes from their ability to be useful in a network. A token's value increases with the number of use cases it has. Utility can take many different forms, such as acting as a means of trade, enabling access to particular features on a platform, or signifying ownership of tangible objects. The general resilience of tokenomics is enhanced by the use cases' variety.

    2.3 Tokenomics and Incentive Structures: Tokenomics incentive structures aim to balance the interests of different stakeholders. Users, developers, miners, and validators are all encouraged to contribute to the security and expansion of the network. Participant rewards in the form of freshly created tokens, transaction fees, or governance rights are frequently used in this. Well-thought-out incentive programs promote a healthy ecology and motivate involvement.

    2.4 Governance Tokens: In many decentralized ecosystems, governance tokens have taken on a crucial role. These coins give holders the ability to suggest and vote on protocol updates, parameter adjustments, and other important decisions, so enabling them to take part in decision-making processes.

    By offering a means of decentralized, community-driven governance, governance tokens strengthen the democratic aspect of decentralized networks.

    2.5 Staking and Yield Farming: Staking is the process of locking up tokens in order to facilitate network functions like block creation and transaction validation. Usually, extra tokens are given to participants. The idea of "yield farming," made popular by DeFi, is users giving liquidity to decentralized exchanges or protocols in return for tokens, or yield. By promoting user engagement, yield farming and staking both strengthen the token economy.

3. Tokenomics's Effect: Molding Decentralized Economies

   3.1 Democratization and Decentralization: A key factor in advancing democratization and decentralization is tokenomics. Token distribution across members can help projects reduce power concentration and decision-making authority. Specifically, governance tokens enable community members to influence the direction of decentralized platforms, promoting a more open and engaged environment.

   3.2 Financial Inclusion: By giving those who were previously shut out of traditional banking systems access to financial services, tokenomics has the potential to improve financial inclusion. Tokenomics-powered DeFi protocols enable users to lend, trade, and borrow without the need for middlemen. This could open up economic prospects for the world's underbanked and unbanked communities.

   3.3 Innovation in Business Models: Decentralized applications and platforms that run on transparent and programmable token economies are the result of tokenomics' invigorating influence on business model innovation. New fundraising techniques like Initial Coin Offerings (ICOs) and Security Token Offerings (STOs), which enable companies to raise cash without the need of traditional financial intermediaries, have been made possible by the capacity to generate and distribute tokens.

   3.4 Liquidity and Market Efficiency: Tokenomics has enhanced liquidity and market efficiency, particularly in the setting of decentralized exchanges and liquidity pools. Users can trade assets straight from their wallets with the use of automated market makers (AMMs) driven by tokenomics, which improves liquidity and makes the market accessible around-the-clock. This also affects conventional financial markets, putting pressure on them to develop more accessible and effective trading systems.

   3.5 dangers and Challenges: Tokenomics has transformed society, but it also contains dangers and challenges. Concerns that need to be addressed are price volatility, security flaws, unclear regulations, and the possibility of market manipulation.

   Resolving these issues is essential to guaranteeing the longevity and broad acceptance of token-based ecosystems as tokenomics develops.

4. Upcoming Patterns and Things to Think About in Tokenomics

   4.1 Integration with Conventional Finance: An emerging trend is the fusion of tokenomics and conventional finance. Security tokens—which adhere to legal conditions. Contractual agreements in traditional finance can entail complicated procedures and middlemen; however, smart contracts automate and streamline these procedures, cutting costs and improving efficiency.

3.2 Coin-Based Token Sales and Initial Coin Offerings (ICOs):
Innovative fundraising techniques like Initial Coin Offerings (ICOs) have been made possible by tokenomics. In contrast to conventional IPOs, initial coin offerings (ICOs) enable enterprises to acquire funds by selling their native tokens to investors directly. The crowdfunding approach has changed the fundraising environment by allowing organizations and companies to access global capital pools without the need for traditional financial middlemen.

3.3 Decentralized Finance (DeFi) Protocols: By providing a variety of financial services without the need for conventional banking infrastructure, DeFi protocols constitute a noteworthy advance in tokenomics. Lending platforms, decentralized exchanges, yield farming, and the production of synthetic assets are examples of these protocols. By doing away with the need for middlemen, DeFi gives consumers more transparency, reduced costs, and control over their financial transactions.

4. **Obstacles and Things to Think About:**
4.1 Regulatory Uncertainties: Regulatory issues have been brought up by the fusion of tokenomics and conventional finance. Global regulatory organizations are facing challenges related to digital asset classification, decentralized platform supervision, and token-based fundraising. It is still difficult to achieve a unified regulatory framework that protects investors while fostering innovation.

4.2 Security Issues and Risks: Tokenomics brings up new security issues, including as the possibility of fraud, hacking, and flaws in smart contracts. Blockchain networks' decentralized structure presents security problems in addition to offering resilience against specific sorts of attacks. To increase public confidence in token-based financial systems, the sector must continuously address and reduce these risks.

4.3 Scalability and Interoperability: As tokenomics grows, these are two increasingly important challenges. Blockchain networks are dealing with a growing volume of transactions; smooth asset transfers require network compatibility. Cross-chain interoperability protocols and layer 2 scaling solutions are two examples of solutions that are currently being developed to address these issues.

5. **Prospective Developments in Conventional Finance and Tokenomics:**

5.1 Integration with Conventional Financial Institutions: Tokenomics will need to become more integrated with conventional financial institutions in the future. Banks and other financial service providers are looking into methods to integrate blockchain technology and digital assets into their business processes as regulatory clarity increases. Hybrid financial systems that incorporate the best aspects of traditional and decentralized finance could result from this merger.

5.2: Central Bank Digital Currencies (CBDCs): CBDCs are a noteworthy advancement at the nexus of traditional finance and tokenomics. A number of central banks are investigating the possibility of issuing virtual currencies through the use of blockchain technology. CBDCs have the ability to close the gap between traditional fiat currencies and digital assets, improve financial inclusion, and modernize payment systems.

5.3 Evolution of Security Tokens: As a means of proving ownership of tangible goods and adhering to legal requirements, security tokens are probably going to become more widely used. These tokens serve as a link between traditional banking and the decentralized world by combining the advantages of tokenization with regulatory compliance. The development of security tokens might open the door to further institutional involvement in tokenized assets.

4.2 Tokenomics and Economic Inclusion

With the potential to address long-standing challenges of economic exclusion, tokenomics—the economic system guiding the production, distribution, and utilization of tokens inside blockchain ecosystems—has become a potent force. This paper investigates the complex relationship between tokenomics and economic inclusion, looking at the ways in which token-based models, digital assets, and decentralized platforms help close gaps in the financial system.

1. **Decentralization: An Engine for Inclusive Economy**

   1.1 Democratizing Financial Services Access: Decentralization is intrinsic to tokenomics, which is based on blockchain technology. The centralized middlemen found in traditional financial systems frequently erect obstacles for those without access to formal banks. Tokenomics-powered Decentralized Finance (DeFi) platforms provide customers access a variety of financial services like borrowing, lending, and trading without depending on conventional gatekeepers. A critical first step toward financial inclusion is the democratization of access to financial services.

   1.2 Encouraging the Underbanked and Unbanked: A sizable section of the world's population does not have access to basic financial services and is either underbanked or unbanked. Because tokenomics is decentralized, anyone can engage in the financial ecosystem without requiring a traditional bank account. By giving those who were previously shut out of the formal financial system the resources they need to manage and expand their finances, inclusion empowers those individuals.

   1.3 Community-Driven Governance: A fundamental element of tokenomics, governance tokens enable users to take part in decentralized networks' decision-making procedures. The establishment and growth of financial protocols is made possible by the community-driven governance, which guarantees the participation of varied voices. Beyond simply providing access to services, economic inclusion entails actively integrating people in the process of establishing the policies that affect their financial situation.

2. **Asset Tokenization: Increasing Investment Possibilities**

    2.1 Dismantling Conventional Barriers: Tokenomics makes it easier to tokenize tangible assets by turning them into programmable tokens. Traditionally illiquid or unattainable assets now have accessibility, liquidity, and divisibility thanks to this process. Tokenization makes investing more accessible by removing these obstacles and enabling a wider spectrum of people to take part in asset ownership and investment opportunities.

    2.2 Accessibility and Fractional Ownership: Tokenization makes it possible for people to hold a portion of valuable assets in fractional ownership. People with low incomes can now invest in precious assets like real estate and artwork because to fractionalization. Regardless of their starting financial situation, people can develop diversified portfolios and accumulate wealth thanks to the inclusivity of investment choices.

    2.3 Worldwide Access to Specialized Assets:
    Non-fungible tokens (NFTs) in particular are digital assets that offer a type of tokenization that goes beyond conventional financial instruments. Ownership of distinctive digital assets, like music, art, and virtual real estate, is made possible via NFTs. Because blockchain networks are global, everyone may invest in and access these exclusive assets from anywhere in the world, promoting economic inclusion in the creative and digital economy.

3. **Financial Inclusion Using Cutting-Edge Token-Based Frameworks**

    3.1 Decentralized Lending and Borrowing: DeFi systems facilitate decentralized lending and borrowing through the use of tokenomics. Assets can be borrowed and lent by users without the assistance of a conventional bank middleman. Those without access to regular banking services or a credit history will be especially affected by this. Economic inclusion is extended to individuals who were previously shut out of the official credit system through decentralized lending.

    3.2 Yield Farming and Staking: Tokenomics presents tools that allow users to lock up their tokens or provide liquidity in exchange for rewards. People can increase their money passively through these actions. In particular, yield farming offers a substitute for conventional savings accounts and lets users profit from their cryptocurrency investments. This model promotes more widespread adoption of wealth-building techniques.

    3.3 Microtransactions and Micropayments: The transmission of extremely little quantities of value is made possible by digital tokens. This is particularly important in areas with lower income levels, as traditional financial institutions would not be able to provide affordable microtransactions. Tokenomics enables people to participate in microtransactions for small-scale trade, internet services, or content consumption, promoting granular economic engagement.

4. **Obstacles and Things to Take Into Account When Advancing Economic Inclusion**

   4.1 User Education and Accessibility: Tokenomics need extensive user education in order to genuinely promote economic inclusiveness. It may be difficult for many people to use decentralized platforms and handle their digital assets, particularly for those who are not familiar with blockchain technology. Expanding the acceptance of token-based financial systems requires making significant improvements to user interfaces, teaching materials, and accessibility.

   4.2 Regulatory Uncertainties: The rules governing tokenomics are still being developed. Adoption of decentralized financial services may be hampered by regulatory uncertainty. It is crucial to strike a balance between innovation and legal compliance so that users of token-based systems can engage with confidence and not worry about facing legal ramifications.

   4.3 Handling Security Issues: As token-based systems proliferate, it is critical to handle security issues. Customers want to know that their funds are safe and that smart contract or decentralized platform risks are minimized. The establishment of industry standards, regular audits, and improved security procedures all help to increase public confidence in token-based financial systems.

5. **Upcoming Trends: Tokenomics to Promote Economic Inclusion**

5.1 Widespread Use of CBDCs: Increasing economic inclusion may be possible with the help of Central Bank Digital Currencies, or CBDCs. As governments examine the issuing of digital currencies, there is a potential to connect CBDCs with decentralized financial systems. Those who depend on digital currencies issued by central banks may find that financial accessibility is improved by this integration.

5.2 Initiatives Based in the Community: Tokenomics-powered community-driven projects have the potential to significantly increase economic inclusion. Initiatives that emphasize adoption at the grassroots level, education, and awareness-raising can help lower barriers and increase the accessibility of decentralized financial services. Encouraging local communities to use token-based systems promotes grassroots economic inclusion.

5.3 Continued Innovation in DeFi: New protocols, financial products, and use cases are constantly being introduced in the decentralized finance area. Subsequent advancements in DeFi can concentrate on streamlining user interfaces even more, enhancing scalability, and launching innovative financial products that serve a wider market. DeFi's capacity to promote economic inclusion will grow as it develops.

4.3 Potential Disruption to Existing Financial Models

There is a chance that the financial structures that are currently in place may be significantly disrupted by tokenomics, the economic system that controls the production, transfer, and use of tokens within blockchain ecosystems. This paper investigates the ways in which tokenomics can disrupt and transform established financial systems. The ramifications of this paradigm shift are extensive and have the capacity to completely alter our understanding of and interactions with financial systems. These include tokenization of assets and decentralized finance (DeFi).

1. **The Potential for Disruption in Decentralized Finance (DeFi):**
   1.1 Decentralized Finance and Debt Management: The rise of DeFi platforms, which facilitate decentralized lending and borrowing, is one of the main disruptions brought about by tokenomics. The exclusive right to provide credit and loans has traditionally been held by established financial institutions like banks. With the use of tokenomics, DeFi breaks up this monopoly by allowing users to lend and borrow money directly through smart contracts, doing away with the necessity for middlemen. In addition to lowering borrowing costs, this disintermediation increases credit availability for people who might not have been able to use traditional banking institutions.
   1.2 Automated Market Makers (AMMs): Another aspect of DeFi that has the ability to upend established financial paradigms is Automated Market Makers (AMMs). Tokenomics is used by these platforms to generate liquidity pools and enable decentralized trading. Wallets allow users to exchange assets directly without depending on centralized exchanges. This strategy upends the established brokerage system and creates new opportunities for people to trade assets effectively and effortlessly around-the-clock, no matter where they are in the world.
   1.3 Yield Farming and Liquidity Mining: New incentive schemes like yield farming and liquidity mining have been brought forth by tokenomics. In conventional financial systems, banks provide interest to customers who deposit money. DeFi systems, on the other hand, use tokenomics to encourage users to add liquidity to the system. Users can gain more tokens as prizes by locking up their tokens in liquidity pools. In addition to upending conventional bank interest rates, this disruptive approach offers consumers other options for asset growth.
2. **Asset Tokenization: Unlocking Novel Opportunities**
   2.1 Tokenization of Real Estate: Tokenomics has made it possible to tokenize assets like real estate that were previously illiquid. Real estate assets can be represented as tokens using blockchain technology, enabling fractional ownership and more liquidity.
   A wider range of people may be able to invest in real estate thanks to this upending of established real estate paradigms, which could democratize access to property.

2.2 Tokenized Securities: Security tokens that represent ownership in conventional financial instruments like stocks and bonds can be created more easily thanks to tokenomics. The process of tokenization improves liquidity and lowers entrance barriers for individual investors. It puts existing stock exchanges to the test by giving people an easier and more effective way to purchase and sell assets, including ones that were once thought to be too complicated or illiquid.

2.3 Art and Collectibles: The art industry has undergone a paradigm shift as a result of the tokenization of art and collectibles using non-fungible tokens (NFTs). With tokenomics, inventors and artists may tokenize their creations and use the blockchain to verify their legitimacy and ownership. Through fractional ownership, this disruption upends established art market systems, giving artists new sources of income and enabling a worldwide audience to engage in the art market.

3. **Obstacles and Things to Think About When There's Disruption:**

    3.1 Uncertainties in Regulation: Tokenomics' disruptive potential presents regulatory challenges as established financial models struggle to keep up with the rise of decentralized systems. Global regulators are striving to create frameworks that balance investor protection with the promotion of innovation. The absence of consistency in rules presents difficulties for companies involved in the tokenomics industry and could hinder the rate of adoption.

    3.2 Security Issues: Although decentralized tokenomics and blockchain systems offer transparency and immutability, they also bring with them new security issues. In the DeFi domain, smart contract flaws, hacks, and possible exploits have been observed. In order to increase confidence in token-based financial systems and stop significant losses, these security issues must be resolved.

    3.3 Integration with Conventional Systems: It is a difficult undertaking to accomplish a smooth integration between tokenomics and conventional financial systems. Significant problems include interoperability, scalability, and compatibility with current infrastructure. Blockchain projects, financial institutions, and regulatory agencies will need to work together and coordinate in order to close the gap between decentralized and centralized finance.

4. **Possible Impact on Financial Intermediaries and Banking:**

    4.1 Obstacles for Conventional Banking: Lending, borrowing, and other financial services provided by DeFi platforms pose a direct threat to banks' conventional function. Users can obtain financial services without depending on conventional banking middlemen by using decentralized alternatives. This change might drastically alter the banking industry, affecting sources of income and forcing established institutions to change how they operate in this new, cutthroat market.

    4.2 Effect on Payment Systems: Tokenomics poses a threat to established payment methods in addition to decentralized finance. Tokenomics-driven cryptocurrencies and stablecoins allow for almost immediate, international transactions at a fraction of the cost of conventional payment methods. The increasing popularity of blockchain-based payment systems presents a possible danger to established payment processors and financial intermediaries.

4.3 The Shifting Functions of Middlemen:
The conventional roles of middlemen in financial transactions are under threat from tokenomics' disruption. The use of smart contracts, automated procedures, and decentralized governance mitigates the necessity for middlemen like clearinghouses, custodians, and brokers. This change could prompt a reassessment of these intermediaries' value offer within the financial ecosystem.

5. **Upcoming Patterns and Adjustment:**

5.1 Central Bank Digital Currencies (CBDCs): In response to tokenomics' potentially disruptive nature, central bank digital currencies, or CBDCs, were created. Central banks are investigating the possibility of issuing virtual currencies in order to keep control over payment systems and monetary policy. Tokenomics and CBDC integration could result in hybrid financial systems that offer the stability and regulatory protection of central banks along with the advantages of decentralized finance.

5.2 Institutional Adoption: The arrival of institutional investors in the cryptocurrency market indicates that tokenomics is becoming more and more accepted. Asset managers, hedge funds, and traditional financial institutions are investigating methods to include digital assets in their portfolios. Increased legitimacy, liquidity, and the creation of new financial products in the tokenomics market could result from this institutional acceptance.

5.3 Regulation Evolution: Tokenomics' future course will be greatly influenced by how regulations develop. Increased clarity and less uncertainty may be experienced by enterprises working in the tokenomics field as regulatory frameworks mature and become more friendly. Token-based systems will require regulatory changes that combine investor protection with innovation in order to thrive sustainably.

Chapter 5

Regulatory Landscape

The financial landscape has undergone a paradigm shift with the introduction of tokenomics, the economic system that regulates the creation, distribution, and use of tokens within blockchain ecosystems. The global authorities are confronted with the task of creating all-encompassing frameworks to control the rapidly changing domains of digital assets, decentralized finance (DeFi), and token-based economies as this revolutionary force gathers pace. This paper investigates the complex and ever-changing regulatory environment around tokenomics, looking at the main obstacles, patterns, and factors that companies, consumers, and regulators need to take into account.

The Changing Character of Regulatory Difficulties

1.1 Defining Digital Assets: The categorization and description of digital assets is one of the main issues facing the tokenomics regulatory environment. It was not the intention of traditional legal frameworks to support the special features of non-fungible tokens (NFTs), utility tokens, security tokens, and cryptocurrencies. The absence of a unified classification makes regulations more difficult to understand and presents obstacles for both market players and regulators.

1.2 Cross-Border Complexity: Tokenomics is a worldwide field that cuts across national borders. But the regulatory environment is dispersed, with many governments treating digital assets in different ways. The absence of uniformity among regulatory frameworks presents difficulties for companies and individuals involved in cross-border dealings and activities. The global regulatory landscape is further complicated by regulatory arbitrage, which is the practice of companies taking advantage of regulatory disparities among nations.

1.3 Decentralized Authority and Management: Many tokenomics projects, especially those in the DeFi area, are decentralized, which makes it difficult to assign accountability and obligation. Banks and regulators are two distinct organizations in traditional financial systems that can be held liable for wrongdoing.

Decentralized networks frequently have community-driven governance, making it more difficult for regulators to enforce compliance and safeguard users. Additionally, fixing problems or vulnerabilities may not always be clear-cut.

2. Global Approaches to Regulation:

2.1 United States: Regulating organizations such as the Securities and Exchange Commission (SEC) are essential to the management of digital assets in the United States. A crucial tool in regulatory decisions is the Howey Test, which evaluates whether an asset meets the requirements to be classified as a security. AML and know your customer (KYC) compliance are the primary areas of attention for the Financial Crimes Enforcement Network (FinCEN), while the Commodity Futures Trading Commission (CFTC) oversees specific parts of digital assets.

2.2 European Union: Efforts have been made by the EU to establish a single regulatory framework for digital assets. A comprehensive framework designed to give legal clarity for the issuance and trading of digital assets is the Markets in Crypto Assets (MiCA) regulation. MiCA offers a standardized regulatory framework that would address issues with market integrity, investor protection, and financial stability in all EU member states.

2.3 Asia-Pacific Area: The nations in the Asia-Pacific area have different policies in place to control tokenomics. Recognized for its progressive outlook, Singapore has created a transparent legal structure for token offers and digital payments. China, on the other hand, has put strong restrictions on initial coin offerings (ICOs) and cryptocurrency trading. Japan has established a licensing mechanism for cryptocurrency exchanges in order to safeguard consumers and maintain the integrity of the industry.

2.4 Switzerland: With the Swiss Financial Market Supervisory Authority (FINMA) offering recommendations for the handling of digital assets, Switzerland has positioned itself as a crypto-friendly state. Switzerland has developed as a center for blockchain and cryptocurrency-related enterprises due to its policy, which emphasizes striking a balance between investor protection and innovation.

3. The Regulatory Landscape's Shaping Trends:

3.1 CBDCs, or Central Bank Digital Currencies: One important development influencing the regulatory environment is the investigation and creation of Central Bank Digital Currencies (CBDCs). In order to improve financial inclusion, update payment systems, and solve the issues raised by private cryptocurrencies, central banks are increasingly thinking of issuing digital currencies.

The way other digital assets are treated will probably change as a result of CBDCs' incorporation into the larger regulatory framework.

3.2 Emphasis on Investor Protection: As the field of tokenomics develops, investor protection is becoming more and more important. To guarantee that market participants are suitably informed about the dangers connected with digital assets, regulatory organizations are implementing measures. To protect investors in this dynamic and frequently volatile market, there has been a shift toward improved disclosure regulations, more transparent token offering guidelines, and increased transparency measures.

3.3 Strengthened KYC and AML Procedures: Global regulators are fortifying their Anti-Money Laundering (AML) and Know Your Customer (KYC) protocols in an effort to reduce the potential for illegal activities linked to digital assets. Strong AML and KYC protocols are becoming more and more necessary for exchanges and platforms that deal with tokens in order to stop financial crimes like money laundering and financing of terrorism.

3.4 Regulatory Sandboxes: To promote innovation while preserving regulatory monitoring, a number of jurisdictions are implementing regulatory sandboxes. These "sandboxes" offer regulated environments in which companies can test new goods and services while being closely monitored by regulators. Regulators can keep up with growing hazards and technical improvements without impeding innovation by using sandboxes.

4. Things to Take Into Account for Companies in the Tokenomics Sector:

4.1 Compliance by Design: Companies operating in the tokenomics market are starting to take a more "compliance by design" stance. This entails incorporating compliance measures from the beginning when designing and developing token-based systems. Businesses can lower their legal risks, increase their credibility, and gain the trust of users and regulators by proactively adhering to regulatory regulations.

4.2 Interaction with Regulators: Businesses navigating the tokenomics landscape must be proactive in their engagement with regulatory organizations. A cooperative relationship between firms and regulators is facilitated by opening channels of communication, requesting regulatory guidance, and taking part in regulatory consultations. Regulators may be better able to comprehend the ramifications of the rapidly changing technology with the aid of such involvement.

4.3 Security and Risk Mitigation: Organizations need to give strong security measures a priority because of the security issues surrounding tokenomics. It is imperative to do periodic security audits, apply optimal techniques for the creation of smart contracts, and guarantee adherence to cybersecurity guidelines. It is essential to reduce the risks associated with fraud, hacking, and vulnerabilities for user safety as well as regulatory compliance.

4.4 Educational programs: As the regulatory environment changes, businesses, regulators, and users all find that educational programs are crucial. Providing instructional materials about the rules and regulations, the need for compliance, and the advantages and disadvantages of using token-based systems promotes an ecosystem that is more responsible and knowledgeable.

5. Prospects and Challenges for the Future:

5.1 Regulatory Harmonization: There is still a long way to go before there is worldwide regulatory harmonization. The lack of uniform regulatory frameworks among jurisdictions makes cross-border activities more difficult and uncertain for users and businesses. Fostering a more unified global regulatory landscape requires the creation of international standards and cooperative efforts toward regulatory harmonization.

5.2 Finding a Tight Balance Between Innovation and Consumer Protection: Regulators constantly have to find a way to safeguard consumers while simultaneously promoting innovation. Because tokenomics is a dynamic industry, regulators must be flexible and keep up with technological developments to protect the interests of users and investors. Attaining this balance is necessary to support an inventive and long-lasting tokenomics environment.

5.3 Adaptation to Technological Developments: Regulators find it difficult to keep up with the quick speed of technological advancements in the tokenomics arena. Regulators must constantly update their knowledge and regulatory strategies in light of emerging technologies like complicated DeFi protocols, non-fungible tokens (NFTs), and decentralized autonomous organizations (DAOs). Regulators need to change with the times to properly handle new opportunities and threats brought about by developing technologies.

5.1 Current Regulatory Environment for FTT

The introduction of Fintech Tokens (FTT) has caused a seismic shift in the fintech sector. These digital assets, which are frequently enabled by blockchain technology, open up new avenues for financial services and bring up issues and concerns for the regulatory environment.

The present regulatory landscape around FTT is examined in this essay, along with the opportunities, trends, and problems that affect regulators and the Fintech industry.

1. **Defining FTTs, or Fintech Tokens:**

   1.1 Features and attributes: Fintech Tokens (FTT) are a class of digital assets created especially for usage with fintech platforms and apps. By utilizing blockchain technology, these tokens enable a range of financial operations, such as loans, payments, remittances, and decentralized finance (DeFi) services. FTTs frequently function as utility tokens, giving users access to particular features inside a financial network.

   1.2 Variety of FTT Types: There are many different kinds of tokens in the FTT area, each with a unique set of applications. Stablecoins are a popular example of fiat money represented on a blockchain. The diverse ecosystem of FTT is enhanced by utility tokens designed for certain financial applications, tokenized assets, and security tokens. Because of its features and functions, each kind has particular regulatory issues.

2. **The Global FTT Regulation Patchwork:**

   2.1 United States: Federal and state governments in the US have different approaches to regulating FTT. Determining if certain FTTs qualify as securities is a critical task for the Securities and Exchange Commission (SEC). A primary focus has been regulatory clarity, and current initiatives seek to create a more lucid framework for differentiating between various token kinds.

2.2 European Union: By combining pre-existing financial rules with specially designed frameworks, the European Union has been aggressively tackling FTT legislation. The Markets in Crypto Assets (MiCA) proposal, which is a component of the larger Digital Finance Package, aims to standardize FTT and other digital asset laws among EU member states. Tokens that are subject to distinct legal requirements, including as utility tokens, e-money tokens, and asset-referenced tokens, are introduced by MiCA.

2.3 Asia-Pacific Area: The nations in the Asia-Pacific area have different approaches to the regulation of FTT. As a fintech hotspot, Singapore has established clear criteria for digital payment tokens and a regulatory sandbox. China has been investigating the usage of digital money issued by its central bank (Digital money Electronic Payment - DCEP), despite restrictions on some cryptocurrency activities. A licensing framework for bitcoin exchanges has been put in place in Japan, with a focus on AML compliance and consumer safety.

2.4 Switzerland: The country has preserved a fintech-friendly atmosphere, offering FTT and blockchain initiatives regulatory clarity. By outlining rules for handling different kinds of tokens, the Swiss Financial Market Supervisory Authority (FINMA) has strengthened the legal environment that fosters fintech innovation.

3. **Regulatory Difficulties and Points to Remember:**

   3.1 Uncertainty in Classification: The difficulty in classifying these tokens is one of the main issues facing FTT in the regulatory framework. The regulatory obligations that apply to FTT projects are greatly impacted by whether they are classified as securities, commodities, or utility tokens. The absence of a unified global classification system adds to the ambiguity around regulations, which impedes both innovation and compliance.

   3.2 AML and KYC Compliance: In the field of financial technology, compliance with AML and KYC regulations is essential. Authorities are eager to make sure that FTT platforms have strong AML and KYC protocols in place to stop illegal activities including financing of terrorism and money laundering. For FTT projects, finding a balance between privacy concerns and regulatory obligations is a difficulty.

   3.3 Smart Contract Audits and Security: To automate financial procedures, smart contracts are frequently used in FTT projects. These smart contracts must be extremely secure because weaknesses can result in cash losses and exploits. The significance of smart contract audits and security procedures in safeguarding users and upholding the integrity of FTT platforms is being emphasized by regulators more and more.

3.4 Cross-Border Operations: Navigating cross-border legislation becomes more difficult due to the global nature of FTT projects. FTT platforms have to take into account the legal needs of many jurisdictions, each of which has a different stance on digital assets. For FTT projects with global operations, balancing these criteria and guaranteeing compliance across borders poses issues.

4. **Developments Affecting FTT Regulation:**
   4.1 Increased Attention to Investor Protection: One notable development in FTT legislation is the increased attention to investor protection. Regulators are attempting to make sure that investors in FTT projects receive equitable treatment, sufficient transparency, and transparent information. The protection of FTT users is further enhanced by strengthened disclosure standards and investor education programs.
   4.2 Regulatory Sandboxes: Fintech companies are increasingly using regulatory sandboxes, which allow them to test new products in a regulated setting. FTT projects can test out new features in these sandboxes under the careful supervision of authorities. The cooperative methodology employed in sandboxes facilitates enhanced comprehension of FTT technologies and their consequences.
   4.3 Integration of CBDCs: FTT regulation is impacted by the way Central Bank Digital Currencies (CBDCs) are included into the financial system. Regulations pertaining to the issuance of digital currency by central banks are changing to allow for the collaboration of CBDCs with private FTT projects. A crucial factor in this tendency is finding a balance between supporting innovation and guaranteeing the stability of the financial system.
   4.4 Industry and Regulators Working Together: The growing cooperation between authorities and the fintech sector is a trend in the right direction. Regulators are conversing with FTT projects, attending conferences and working groups, and getting feedback from industry stakeholders. The goal of this cooperative approach is to create legislative frameworks that manage possible risks and encourage innovation.
5. **Things to Think About for FTT Companies:**
   5.1 Regulatory Compliance by Design: FTT companies should incorporate compliance safeguards into the conception and creation of their platforms in order to take a proactive stance toward regulatory compliance. This entails making certain that smart contracts are routinely audited, privacy concerns are taken care of right away, and AML and KYC protocols are strong.
   5.2 Engagement with authorities: FTT firms must navigate the regulatory landscape by being proactive in their engagement with authorities. Building a cooperative relationship involves asking for regulatory guidance, holding open channels of communication, and taking part in regulatory discussions. In order to improve comprehension, FTT companies might give authorities insights into

their operational methods and technology.

5.3 Security and Privacy Measures: Businesses need to give the adoption of strong security measures top priority because FTT regulations place a strong emphasis on security and privacy. Establishing confidence with regulators and users is facilitated by conducting regular security audits, adhering to best practices in smart contract creation, and demonstrating a commitment to user privacy.

5.4 Global Regulatory Compliance: Companies that provide financial technology and have global operations need to manage the challenges of global regulatory compliance. This entails keeping up with changes in regulations across several jurisdictions, adjusting to new needs, and formulating plans to coordinate cross-border compliance initiatives.

6. **Prospects and Challenges for the Future:**

6.1 Harmonization of International Regulations: It is still very difficult to harmonize international FTT regulations. The absence of uniform frameworks among jurisdictions leads to regulatory fragmentation, impeding the smooth functioning of FTT platforms worldwide. To meet this problem, international cooperation and the creation of uniform standards are needed.

6.2 Technical Development and Regulatory Adaptation: Regulators continue to face difficulties in keeping up with the quick speed of technology improvements in the fintech industry. Innovative alternatives including non-fungible tokens (NFTs), decentralized finance (DeFi), and sophisticated smart contract features are being investigated by FTT initiatives. Regulators need to keep up with these advances in order to handle opportunities and dangers in an efficient manner.

6.3 Innovation and Regulatory Certainty in Balance:

Finding a balance between encouraging innovation and offering regulatory certainty is important for the future. Regulators must ensure that FTT projects follow well-defined and predictable regulatory rules while also modifying frameworks to account for technological improvements. Maintaining this equilibrium is necessary to support a vibrant and ethical fintech sector.

5.2 Challenges and Opportunities

The nexus of digital tokens and financial technology is known as the Fintech Token (FTT) ecosystem, and it is developing quickly. The emergence of this innovative ecosystem presents a range of opportunities and difficulties that influence the direction of FTT projects, legal frameworks, and user experiences. This paper explores the complex environment of opportunities and constraints in the FTT ecosystem, looking at how stakeholders manage complexities to take advantage of potentially game-changing breakthroughs.

1. **Difficulties in the FTT Environment:**
   1.1 Regulatory ambiguity: In the FTT ecosystem, regulatory ambiguity is

still a recurring problem. The wide range of FTT classifications—from security tokens to utility tokens—leads to regulatory framework ambiguities. Fintech projects frequently struggle to achieve compliance and regulatory clarity as regulatory agencies struggle to comprehend and adjust to the dynamic nature of FTT.

These concerns are made worse by the absence of globally standardized rules, which makes it more difficult for FTT platforms to operate seamlessly across borders.

1.2 Privacy and Security Issues: The security and privacy aspects of FTT are brought about by the decentralized and encrypted nature of blockchain technology. Users and FTT projects are at serious risk from data breaches, hacking attacks, and vulnerabilities in smart contracts. In the FTT ecosystem, ensuring smart contract security through routine audits, putting strong encryption in place, and attending to privacy issues are constant problems. Maintaining a delicate equilibrium between privacy and transparency is still a difficult task.

1.3 Compliance and Cross-Border Operations: Because the FTT ecosystem is global in scope, operations must take place in several jurisdictions, each with its own set of regulations. For FTT projects, navigating cross-border compliance presents a difficult task that necessitates a deep comprehension of various legal and regulatory environments. A significant challenge for FTT platforms with global operations is to balance compliance efforts while accommodating divergent regulatory requirements.

1.4 Innovation and Technological Complexity: Both opportunities and disadvantages are brought about by the FTT ecosystem's high speed of technological advancement. Projects are faced with the challenges of safely integrating technologies such as non-fungible tokens (NFTs), advanced smart contract functionality, and decentralized finance (DeFi). To remain at the forefront of innovation, FTT initiatives face obstacles including as interoperability issues, scalability difficulties, and the need for constant adaption to emerging technology.

1.5 User Education and acceptance: User comprehension and acceptance are essential for the smooth integration of FTT into traditional financial services. It's possible that a large number of potential customers are unfamiliar with digital wallets, blockchain technology, and the nuances of FTT features. For FTT initiatives hoping to spur widespread adoption and improve user experiences, closing this knowledge gap, streamlining user interfaces, and putting in place successful instructional programs are critical obstacles to be overcome.

2. **Possibilities inside the FTT Environment:**

    2.1 Financial Inclusion: The FTT ecosystem has a number of opportunities, one of which is its capacity to promote financial inclusion. By overcoming conventional banking constraints, FTT initiatives can give underbanked or unbanked people access to financial services.

FTT can provide financial services to a worldwide population that has been previously underserved by established financial systems by utilizing decentralized platforms and blockchain technology.

2.2 Innovation in Decentralized Finance (DeFi): Within the FTT ecosystem, Decentralized Finance (DeFi) offers a revolutionary prospect. Without the use of conventional middlemen, DeFi platforms powered by FTT provide a variety of financial services like lending, borrowing, and trading. The removal of middlemen improves productivity, lowers expenses, and creates a financial ecosystem that is more inclusive. DeFi innovation gives FTT projects additional ways to influence how finance develops in the future.

2.3 Asset Tokenization: Within the FTT ecosystem, tokenizing tangible goods presents a large opportunity. FTT initiatives can make it easier to represent tangible assets on a blockchain as digital tokens, including real estate or commodities. This procedure increases investment opportunities, facilitates fractional ownership, and improves liquidity. Tokenization helps to democratize asset ownership by making it possible for more people to engage in marketplaces that were previously closed to outsiders.

2.4 Effective Cross-Border Transactions: FTT initiatives can improve cross-border transactions by utilizing blockchain technology, which provides speed, affordability, and transparency. In contrast to conventional banking systems, FTT-powered stablecoins and cryptocurrencies allow for almost immediate, international transactions. By addressing the difficulties involved in cross-border payments, this possibility improves the efficiency and accessibility of financial transactions on an international level.

2.5 Smart Contracts for Automation: The FTT ecosystem's incorporation of smart contracts offers chances for efficiency and automation. Self-executing contracts known as "smart contracts" that follow pre-established guidelines can simplify a number of financial operations, such as trading, lending, and borrowing. Automation lowers human error, eliminates the need for middlemen, and improves the overall effectiveness of financial processes within the FTT ecosystem.

3. **Finding a Balance: Handling Difficulties while Seizing Chances:**

3.1 Regulatory Cooperation and Advocacy: Cooperation and advocacy are necessary to address regulatory problems in the FTT ecosystem. FTT initiatives, trade groups, and authorities can have productive discussions to create frameworks that strike a balance between innovation, investor safety, and market integrity. By proactively interacting with authorities, FTT initiatives can offer valuable insights that promote a more sophisticated comprehension of the technology and its consequences.

3.2 Strengthening Security Measures: FTT projects need to provide strong security measures top priority in order to allay security worries. Establishing trust with users and regulators is facilitated by conducting regular security audits, adhering to best practices in the construction of smart contracts, and making continuous efforts to stay ahead of cybersecurity threats. Enhancing the entire security posture of the ecosystem can be achieved by collaborative initiatives within the FTT community to share security best practices.

3.3 User Education Initiatives: Targeted educational initiatives are necessary to overcome obstacles in user education. To introduce consumers to the features and advantages of FTT, projects might fund community outreach, educational materials, and user-friendly interfaces. Through de-mystifying blockchain technology and streamlining onboarding procedures, FTT initiatives can promote wider adoption and cultivate an informed and empowered user base.

3.4 Cross-Border Collaboration: Cross-border cooperation is essential for navigating cross-border compliance issues. FTT projects have the ability to interact with regulatory bodies in many jurisdictions, requesting advice and setting up compliance frameworks that meet a range of regulatory requirements. Global regulatory framework for FTT is becoming more unified as a result of cooperation amongst international organizations, industry participants, and regulators.

3.5 Constant Innovation and Adaptation: The FTT ecosystem's dynamic character necessitates constant innovation and adaptation. FTT initiatives are better positioned to take advantage of opportunities when they aggressively embrace evolving technologies, investigate novel use cases, and tackle issues related to scalability and interoperability. By remaining on the cutting edge of innovation, FTT projects have the ability to influence the changing environment and add to the larger story of the fintech revolution.

5.3 Future Regulatory Trends

Regulating frameworks are attempting to keep up with the quick advances in financial technology as the Fintech Token (FTT) ecosystem develops. Future legislative developments in the FTT sector will have a significant impact on how investors, customers, and FTT projects are positioned. This paper investigates prospective regulatory developments that could materialize in the upcoming years, examining the opportunities and problems they raise as well as their effects on the larger financial ecosystem.

1. **Harmonization of FTT Regulations Worldwide:**

    1.1 The Fragmentation Challenge: At the moment, the regulatory environment around FTT is typified by a patchwork of various standards and methodologies used by various authorities. FTT initiatives face difficulties because they frequently function on a worldwide scale due to the absence of global harmonization. Regulation fragmentation can make it more difficult to comply with the law, create legal uncertainty, and make it more difficult for FTT platforms to operate seamlessly across borders.

1.2 Moving Towards Common Criteria: A coordinated push for international harmonization may be a future trend in FTT regulation. International organizations and regulators may work together to create uniform guidelines for FTT trading, issuance, and classification. Harmonized laws would simplify the framework for FTT projects, ease the burden of compliance, and promote a more effective and integrated global FTT ecosystem.

1.3 Cooperation Among Regulatory Bodies: To solve the difficulties posed by cross-border FTT operations, regulators from various jurisdictions may work together more and more. To improve information exchange between regulatory authorities and expedite regulatory procedures, bilateral and multilateral agreements might be created. Such cooperation would demonstrate a change in the regulatory landscape toward one that is more cooperative and recognizes the international scope of FTT operations.

2. **Improved Token Classification Regulatory Clarity:**

    2.1 Clearly Defined Criteria: One of the most important parts of regulation is still classifying FTTs into groups like utility tokens, security tokens, and payment tokens. In the future, regulators might establish uniform and transparent standards for these divisions. To help FTT projects comprehend the regulations that apply to their tokens, clear rules would be helpful. They would also allow investors to base their judgments on standardized information and make well-informed choices.

    2.2 Dynamic Frameworks for Changing Tokens: Future regulatory trends may entail the creation of frameworks that can change to accommodate token functionalities, considering the FTT ecosystem's dynamic character. The implementation of systems for frequent assessments and updates by regulators can guarantee the continued relevance of regulatory classifications in the face of technological changes. This flexibility would help create a regulatory environment that is more responsive and flexible.

3. **A focus on education and investor protection**

    3.1 Disclosure Requirements and Transparency: Investor protection will probably be given more weight in future regulatory developments. To guarantee that investors receive clear and thorough information, regulators may impose stricter disclosure standards for FTT projects. A more knowledgeable investor base may result from clearer regulations on risk disclosure, project documentation, and financial reporting.

    3.2 Educational efforts: To improve public knowledge and comprehension of FTTs, regulators may fund educational efforts. Education campaigns could be directed at consumers, investors, and even financial experts in order to guarantee a more comprehensive comprehension of the advantages and disadvantages of participating in the FTT ecosystem. Regulators hope to enable customers to

Chapter 6

Risks And Security Concerns

Driven by cutting-edge technology such as blockchain, the Fintech Token (FTT) ecosystem has transformed financial environments by bringing about novel opportunities and conveniences. But these developments also bring with them security issues and hazards that need to be carefully considered. In order to protect the safety and integrity of FTT projects and their stakeholders, this essay looks at the wide range of hazards that are common in the FTT ecosystem and investigates ways to reduce these worries.

1. An overview of the FTT ecosystem's risks

    1.1 Market Volatility and Speculative Risks: FTTs' vulnerability to market volatility is one of the main risks they face. Users and investors may become uneasy due to speculative actions brought on by the volatile values of tokens and cryptocurrencies. Fast price fluctuations, which are frequently impacted by outside events and market mood, present financial risks and have the ability to cause substantial losses.

    1.2 Dangers of Regulation and Compliance: Projects operating in many jurisdictions have compliance problems because to the dynamic regulatory environment around FTTs. Regulations that are too strict or unclear, sudden changes in regulations, and noncompliance with regulations can lead to penalties, fines, or even the closure of business. FTT platforms are made more sophisticated and exposed to more risk due to regulatory concerns.

    1.3 Hacking Risks and Cybersecurity Vulnerabilities: Blockchain and FTT projects are not immune to cybersecurity concerns due to their decentralized nature. There are serious risks associated with phishing attempts, exchange hacking, and smart contract flaws. Financial losses, compromised user data, and harm to the reputation of FTT platforms can result from exploits or breaches, which also erode confidence.

    1.4 Operational Risks and Technology Failures: FTT projects are vulnerable to operational risks brought on by malfunctions in the infrastructure or by technical failures, system outages, or interruptions.

Smart contract problems, network congestion, or inadequate scalability can all cause operational disruptions that affect user experiences and result in losses of money. Dependence on intricate technologies demands strong backup strategies to handle operational hazards.

1.5 Scams and Fraudulent Activities: Because blockchain identities are pseudonymous and transactions are anonymous, fraudsters can easily operate in this environment. Investors who aren't cautious are at risk from Ponzi schemes, pump-and-dump schemes, and fraudulent claims of substantial profits. In some situations, a lack of regulatory control makes the FTT ecosystem more susceptible to scams.

2. **Security Issues with FTT Initiatives:**

   2.1 Vulnerabilities in Smart Contracts: Smart contracts, which are essential to FTT projects, are prone to vulnerabilities and coding flaws. Reentrancy attacks and logic defects, among other flaws in smart contract code, can result in the theft, exploitation, or even total loss of cash. To reduce this risk, auditing and testing smart contracts for vulnerabilities is crucial.

   2.2 Exchange and Wallet Security: FTT holders are exposed to a significant risk from security breaches in exchanges and wallets. Centralized exchanges could be the subject of hacking attempts, which could result in large financial losses. Similar to this, flaws in custodial or digital wallet systems may allow private keys to be compromised and grant illegal access to funds. Securing assets requires strong security protocols, such as multi-factor authentication and encryption.

   2.3 Phishing and Social Engineering Attacks: Phishing attacks try to trick users into divulging private keys or login credentials by having malicious parties pose as trustworthy websites or organizations. Social engineering techniques take advantage of people's weaknesses to trick them into inadvertently jeopardizing their security. To mitigate these hazards, education and awareness initiatives are essential for spotting phishing attempts and avoiding social engineering.

3. **Reducing Hazards in the FTT Environment:**

   3.1 Regulatory Compliance and Risk Management: Adherence to changing regulatory frameworks must be given top priority in FTT initiatives. One way to reduce the risks associated with noncompliance with regulations is to have strong risk management procedures. Navigating regulatory complexity requires proactive engagement with authorities, regular compliance audits, and the implementation of internal controls.

   3.2 Cybersecurity Best Practices: To reduce cybersecurity risks, implementing strong cybersecurity measures is essential. Regular security assessments, the use of encryption technologies, and the adoption of secure coding techniques for smart contracts are all recommended for FTT initiatives. Steps that are critical to strengthening defenses against cyber threats include timely patching of security gaps and continuous vulnerability monitoring.

3.3 Initiatives for Education and Awareness: Improving investors' and consumers' knowledge of the dangers posed by FTTs is essential to risk mitigation. In order to improve users' comprehension of security best practices, spot potential frauds, and protect their money, FTT initiatives should offer thorough and easily available training tools. An informed and watchful community benefits from increased user awareness.

3.4 Due Diligence and Transparency: In FTT initiatives, investors and users alike benefit from transparency and due diligence. Platforms should make all of their operational details, including project paperwork, audits, and governance frameworks, readily available. Clear disclosure about possible dangers and weaknesses promotes trustworthiness and aids in decision-making for users.

3.5 Continuous Improvement and Adaptation: To handle new risks, FTT initiatives must adopt a culture of continuous improvement and adaptation. Keeping ahead of developing threats requires putting feedback systems into place, keeping up with technical developments, and iteratively improving security measures. Resilient FTT ecosystems require swift adaptation to shifting risk environments.

Collaborative Attempts and Industry Proposals:

4.1 Industry Collaboration for Security Standards: The development of best practices and industry-wide security standards can result from cooperative efforts within the FTT sector. The sharing of knowledge, materials, and security procedures can be facilitated by industry groups, coalitions, or forums. By facilitating coordinated responses to new threats, collaborative actions improve the ecosystem's overall security posture.

4.2 Regulatory-Industry Partnerships and Dialogue: Addressing security problems requires collaboration between regulators and FTT industry players. Mutual understanding is fostered via discussions, working groups, and collaborations between regulatory agencies and FTT projects. While FTT initiatives can provide insights into technology improvements, regulators can offer advise and aid in the building of effective regulatory frameworks.

6.1 Security Challenges in Tokenomics

The fundamental component of decentralized systems and blockchain networks is tokenomics, the economic theory that controls the production, transfer, and administration of tokens. Maintaining confidence, encouraging adoption, and protecting the integrity of the ecosystem as a whole depend heavily on the security of tokenomics as digital assets become more commonplace. This paper investigates the complex terrain of tokenomics security issues, focusing on the weak points, dangers, and defense mechanisms for digital assets.

Smart Contract Deficiencies:

1.1 Tokenomics' Core Principles: Tokenomics revolves around smart contracts, which are self-executing agreements with coded terms. They streamline procedures like token distribution, transfers, and governance in blockchain networks and decentralized apps (DApps). Smart contracts can still be vulnerable, though. Coding mistakes, oversights, or gaps might result in exploitable vulnerabilities, jeopardizing the tokenomic system's overall security.

1.2 Common Vulnerabilities in Smart Contracts: Reentrancy attacks, in which an external contract takes advantage of a loop in the target contract, and integer overflow/underflow, in which arithmetic operations surpass the bounds of variable types, are examples of common vulnerabilities. Inadequate input validation, unauthorized external calls, and poor access control can also result in attack vectors. Malicious actors might be able to take advantage of these vulnerabilities to alter token balances, carry out unlawful transactions, or interfere with tokenomic operations.

1.3 Mitigation Strategies: To find and fix smart contract vulnerabilities, thorough code reviews and regular security audits are crucial. Hiring outside security specialists or smart contract auditing companies helps guarantee a comprehensive analysis and offers an outside viewpoint. To improve the robustness of smart contracts, developers should follow best practices, make use of well-established libraries, and use formal verification techniques.

2. Centralized Failure Points:

2.1 Exchanges and Custodial Risks: One common aspect of tokenomics is the trading of tokens via centralized marketplaces. Custodial services and centralized exchanges create a single point of failure. The tokenomic ecosystem's overall security and trustworthiness may be impacted by user funds being compromised due to security lapses, hacking, or improper handling of private keys in centralized exchanges.

2.2 Mitigation Techniques: Non-custodial wallets and decentralized exchanges (DEXs) provide substitutes that lessen the dangers of centralized points of failure. In non-custodial wallets, users maintain ownership over their private keys, which lessens reliance on centralized organizations. Decentralized finance (DeFi) systems are continuing to progress, offering more ways for consumers to participate in tokenomic activities without depending on conventional centralized exchanges.

3. Difficulties with Regulatory Compliance:

3.1 Uncertainty in the Regulatory Environment: Tokenomics regulations are still evolving and differ greatly between countries. The absence of well-defined and uniform legislation presents obstacles for token economy initiatives. Legal risks can arise from regulatory uncertainties because projects may unintentionally violate compliance standards or encounter shifting regulatory expectations.

3.2 Mitigation Strategies: Tokenomic projects attempting to negotiate the intricate regulatory landscape must collaborate with legal professionals and regulatory specialists. Mitigating legal risks can be achieved through proactive engagement with regulatory organizations, participation in regulatory sandboxes when appropriate, and adherence to current financial regulations. Projects need to keep up with changing rules so they can modify their tokenomics models appropriately.

4. **Oracle Hazards and External Dependencies:**

    4.1 Dependency on External Data Feeds: For real-time data, a lot of decentralized apps and smart contracts rely on external data sources or oracles. The hazards associated with external dependencies stem from the potential for manipulation or compromise of the accuracy and reliability of data derived from oracles.

    4.2 Mitigation Strategies: To improve the security of tokenomic systems, numerous oracles can be implemented, decentralized oracle networks can be used, and cryptographic techniques can be used to check data integrity. One way to reduce the risks associated with external dependencies is to introduce fail-safes, like time-locked smart contracts, and establish clear rules for resolving discrepancies in data feeds.

5. **Issues with Anonymity and Privacy:**

    5.1 Transactions on Blockchain Are Often Pseudonymous: Although blockchain transactions are pseudonymous, they are not totally private. Transaction traceability is made possible by blockchain ledgers' transparency. It is difficult for users who value secrecy in their tokenomic actions to deal with this loss of privacy.

    5.2 Strategies for Mitigation: By improving transaction privacy, privacy-focused technologies like zero-knowledge proofs and privacy coins seek to overcome these obstacles. Projects that integrate privacy features or collaborate with privacy-focused solutions give customers more options for transacting in a more anonymous manner.

6. **Scalability and Congestion in the Network:**

    6.1 Scalability Issues: As decentralized applications and blockchain networks gain traction, scalability poses a serious problem. The effectiveness and user experience of tokenomic systems can be negatively impacted by network congestion and expensive transaction fees, which may deter general adoption.

    6.2 Mitigation Strategies: By offloading some transactions from the main blockchain, layer-2 scaling solutions like state channels and sidechains assist reduce congestion. By increasing throughput and lowering transaction fees, blockchain networks are being developed with the goal of addressing scalability issues. One such project is Ethereum, which is currently evolving into Ethereum 2.0.

7. **Interoperability is lacking:**

    7.1 Fragmented Ecosystems: Ecosystems get fragmented due to a lack of compatibility across various blockchain networks and token standards. When interacting with decentralized apps that run on various blockchains or transferring assets between platforms, users could run into difficulties.

7.2 Mitigation Strategies: Interoperability standards like the Interledger Protocol (ILP) and cross-chain bridges allow for easy asset transfers between different blockchain networks. Interoperability-focused projects help to build a tokenomic environment that is more unified and user-friendly.

8. **Risks Associated with Community Governance:**

8.1 Decentralized Governance Challenges: Decentralized governance solutions, which let token holders take part in decision-making, are frequently used in tokenomic initiatives. Nevertheless, there are drawbacks to decentralized governance, like voter apathy, manipulation, or the consolidation of power in the hands of a small number of powerful token holders.

8.2 Mitigation Strategies: You can improve the efficacy and fairness of decentralized governance by putting in place clear governance frameworks, promoting extensive token holder participation, and using techniques like quadratic voting. To handle new issues, projects should seek input from their communities, actively engage with them, and refine their governance models.

6.2 Fraud and Hacking Risks

The field of tokenomics is becoming more vulnerable to fraud and hacking hazards as the use of digital assets increases. Malicious actors aim to take advantage of the vulnerabilities introduced by the decentralized nature of blockchain technology and the inventive structures of tokenomics. This essay explores the numerous dangers related with tokenomics components and solutions to manage them, delving into the complex issues raised by fraud and hacking in the digital asset ecosystem.

1. **The Challenging Landscape of Fraud and Cybersecurity Risks:**

    1.1 Token Theft and Unauthorized Access: Theft of tokens by unapproved access to wallets or exchanges is a common danger in tokenomics. Malicious actors use a variety of strategies, such as keyloggers, phishing assaults, and platform vulnerabilities that they can exploit to obtain private keys or user credentials, which allows them to move digital assets without authorization.

    1.2 Smart Contract Exploits: If smart contracts are not carefully developed and audited, they can be exploited. Smart contracts are essential to many tokenomic systems. Smart contract vulnerabilities may be used to carry out illicit transactions, modify token balances, or enable fraudulent operations in blockchain networks and decentralized apps (DApps).

    1.3 Market Manipulation and Pump-and-Dump Schemes: Market manipulation is a type of fraudulent activity in which unscrupulous parties take advantage of liquidity and fabricate demand in order to manipulate token values.

Pump-and-dump methods include coordinated purchases to artificially inflate the price of a token, which is then hastily sold off, leaving unwary investors with depreciated assets.

1.4 Identity Theft and Impersonation: In the realm of digital assets, identity theft refers to the unlawful exploitation of personal data to assume the identity of people or organizations. Malevolent entities may assume the guise of reputable entities or persons, tricking users into divulging confidential data or engaging in illicit token economy operations.

2. **Taking Care of Wallet Security**

    2.1 Centralized Exchange Risks: Centralized exchanges offer a centralized point of failure in addition to liquidity and simplicity of trade. User money may be compromised as a result of security lapses in these transactions. The necessity for strong security measures to safeguard user assets has been highlighted by well-publicized attacks on centralized systems.

    2.2 Vulnerabilities with Decentralized Wallets: Hackers may attempt to access decentralized wallets, particularly those that are run by people who don't place a high priority on security. Users may be vulnerable to asset theft and illegal access due to weak password protection, flaws in private keys, or insufficient encryption protection.

    2.3 Hardware Wallet Security: Because hardware wallets store private keys offline, they are thought to be more secure than software wallets. Even so, there are still risks associated with these gadgets. The security of hardware wallets might be jeopardized by supply chain intrusions, hardware component weaknesses, or tampering, which highlights the significance of choosing reliable suppliers and updating firmware.

3. **Reducing the Risk of Smart Contracts:**

    3.1 Smart Contract Audits: Thorough auditing by security professionals is required for the implementation of smart contracts. Audits of smart contracts find bugs in the code, potential exploits, and vulnerabilities. The overall security of smart contracts is improved by using community-driven audits or third-party auditing organizations, which lowers the possibility of flaws being exploited.

    3.2 Smart Contract Security Best Practices:

    It is essential that security best practices be followed when creating smart contracts. This entails applying secure coding standards, staying away from needless complexity, and making use of well-known libraries. The development of features that allow developers to upgrade or halt contracts in reaction to vulnerabilities found must be given top priority.

    3.3 Bug Bounty Programs: Tokenomic projects have the option to set up bug bounty programs in order to promote the discovery of such vulnerabilities. Security researchers and ethical hackers are encouraged by these schemes to find and report vulnerabilities in exchange for prizes. Bug bounty programs help identify possible vulnerabilities before malevolent actors do and support continuous security enhancements.

4. **Countering Market Deception:**

   4.1 Enhanced Surveillance and Monitoring: In order to identify anomalous trade patterns suggestive of market manipulation, exchanges and regulatory authorities need to put in place enhanced surveillance and monitoring technologies. Real-time monitoring of trading activity is helpful in spotting and averting pump-and-dump scams, particularly when there is substantial price volatility.

   4.2 Reporting and Transparency Requirements:
   Fighting market manipulation is aided by regulations that enforce reporting obligations and transparency. Tokenomic initiatives and exchanges should follow disclosure guidelines and give users accurate and comprehensible information. Clear disclosure of trading volumes and token economy activity promotes a more reliable and knowledgeable market.

5. **Fortifying Identity Confirmation:**

   5.1 Two-Factor Authentication (2FA): Improving identity verification requires using two-factor authentication (2FA). Beyond passwords, 2FA adds an extra degree of protection by asking users to authenticate themselves using a secondary method—like a text message or mobile app.

   5.2 Biometric Authentication: Technological developments make it possible to improve identity verification procedures by integrating biometric authentication, such as fingerprint or facial recognition. When properly preserved, biometric data adds another level of protection, making it more difficult for bad actors to pose as users.

   5.3 Decentralized Identity Solutions: By utilizing blockchain technology, decentralized identity solutions provide consumers authority over their personal data. By lowering the reliance on centralized databases and lowering the possibility of significant data breaches, these technologies improve privacy and security.

6. **Interoperability, Security, and Scalability:**

   6.1 Scalability Solutions: By putting scaling solutions into place, scalability issues—which are frequently made worse by spikes in demand—can be resolved. Techniques like layer-2 solutions, sidechains, and sharding are a few examples of how to improve the efficiency and throughput of blockchain networks while lowering the chance of delays and congestion.

   6.2 Interoperability Protocols: Interoperability protocols are essential for reducing the dangers that come with ecosystem fragmentation. Cross-chain bridges and the Interledger Protocol (ILP) are two standards that make it easier to transfer assets between blockchain networks. Interoperability-focused projects help create a more robust and interconnected token economy.

7. **Educating and Giving Users Power:**

   7.1 User Education Initiatives: Tokenomic projects ought to fund extensive user education programs to increase knowledge of possible hazards and security best practices.

Users should have easy access to tutorials, resources, and educational content so they may safely traverse the world of digital assets and make educated decisions.

7.2 Community Engagement: Establishing a collaborative approach to security and fostering trust are fostered by actively engaging the community through official channels, social media, and forums. Clear and open communication regarding security protocols, current trends, and possible hazards motivates users to exercise caution and engage in the joint endeavor of upholding a safe tokenomic environment.

8. **Coordination and Regulatory Actions:**

8.1 Regulatory Frameworks: In the context of digital assets, regulatory organizations are essential in reducing the dangers of fraud and hacking. Well-defined and all-encompassing regulatory structures offer legal protection and discourage malevolent actions. An ecosystem for tokenomics that is safe and compliant is established by projects that follow regulations.

8.2 International Cooperation: Since digital assets are worldwide in scope, international cooperation amongst regulatory agencies is crucial. Working together can reduce the dangers of international fraud and hacking, make information sharing easier, and build unified standards that will make the ecosystem more uniform and safe for users and tokenomic initiatives.

6.3 Mitigation Strategies and Best Practices

It is becoming more and more important to protect tokenomics from fraud, possible dangers, and cyber threats as the environment of digital assets changes. To strengthen the foundations of tokenomics, this essay examines a wide range of mitigation techniques and best practices. The digital asset ecosystem can support a safe and resilient tokenomic environment by resolving vulnerabilities, putting strong security measures in place, and encouraging user education and regulatory compliance.

1. **Security of Smart Contracts:**

    1.1 Comprehensive Audits: Smart contracts, which are essential to many tokenomic systems, need to go through comprehensive security audits carried out by reliable outside companies. By finding vulnerabilities, code mistakes, and possible exploits, these audits make sure smart contracts are reliable and strong. Frequent audits are a fundamental security safeguard, especially prior to the implementation of new contracts or modifications.

    1.2 Code Evaluations and Ideal Procedures: When developing smart contracts, it's imperative to use secure coding techniques. Expert developers' code reviews assist in locating and fixing possible vulnerabilities. Following accepted best practices makes smart contracts less vulnerable to common vulnerabilities and code flaws. One example of such a practice is the ConsenSys Smart Contract Best Practices.

1.3 Bug reward Programs: Tokenomic projects ought to think about putting in place bug reward programs to encourage security researchers and ethical hackers among other members of the community to find and disclose flaws. These tools can be crucial in identifying possible vulnerabilities before malevolent parties do, advancing the continuous enhancement of smart contract security.

2. **Security of Wallets:**

   2.1 Promote Hardware Wallets: Promoting hardware wallets among users improves private key security. By storing private keys offline, hardware wallets lower the possibility of being vulnerable to online attacks. Initiatives can instruct users on the advantages of hardware wallets and offer security best practices.

   2.2 Multi-Signature Wallets: By requiring multiple private keys to authorize a transaction, multi-signature (multisig) wallets add an additional degree of protection. Because transactions cannot be completed with just compromised passwords or private keys, this lowers the possibility of illegal access. Multisig wallets are very important for projects whose governance systems are complicated.

   2.3 Informing Users of Recommended Practices:
   One essential element of wallet security is user education. Projects should give customers easy-to-understand educational materials that instruct them on the best ways to secure their wallets. The significance of using strong passwords, frequent updates, and avoiding phishing efforts are a few possible topics.

3. **Adherence to Regulations:**

   3.1 Consulting with Legal professionals: Legal professionals and consultants with a focus on blockchain and digital assets are necessary to navigate the regulatory environment. Legal experts can offer perceptions into changing regulatory environments, guaranteeing that tokenomic initiatives comply with legal needs and operate legally.

   3.2 Proactive Regulatory Communication: Tokenomic projects ought to communicate with regulatory organizations in a proactive manner. This may entail getting legal advice, taking part in regulatory sandboxes when they're accessible, and keeping lines of communication open. Projects are better positioned for compliance when a collaborative approach is used to promote a greater grasp of regulatory expectations.

   3.3 Constantly Tracking Regulatory Developments: Regular updates and modifications are made to the dynamic regulatory environment. Projects need to set up systems for tracking changes in regulations over time. Proactive modifications to tokenomic models and operations are made possible by remaining up to date on changes in laws and regulations.

4. **KYC and Identity Verification:**

   4.1 Applying KYC Policies: Know Your Customer (KYC) policies aid in the verification of identification and aid in the suppression of fraud. Initiatives that apply KYC protocols, especially for large-scale transactions or user engagements, improve the overall security and credibility of their token economy ecosystems.

4.2 Biometric Authentication: Identity verification procedures are improved by incorporating biometric authentication, such as fingerprint or facial recognition. When properly preserved, biometric data adds another level of protection, making it more difficult for bad actors to pose as users.

4.3 Decentralized Identity Solutions: By utilizing blockchain technology, decentralized identity solutions provide consumers authority over their personal data. By lowering reliance on centralized databases, these solutions improve security and privacy while lowering the possibility of significant data breaches brought on by more conventional identity verification techniques.

5. **Education and Community Involvement:**

    5.1 Transparent Communication: It is imperative that projects give their communities' transparent communication top priority. Transparency and trust are fostered by regular updates on security measures, continuing developments, and potential concerns. Vigilant and knowledgeable users are developed through open and sincere conversation.

    5.2 Educational programs: In order to empower users, extensive educational programs must be established. Projects should include easily obtainable tutorials, educational materials, and content on subjects like safe wallet procedures, spotting phishing scams, and comprehending the dangers of tokenomic activity.

    5.3 Community Feedback Mechanisms: In order to get community insights, tokenomic projects can have feedback mechanisms in place. Users are more likely to feel involved in continuing security efforts when a collaborative environment is fostered by actively seeking input, addressing problems, and incorporating community feedback into security standards.

6. **Solutions for Scalability and Interoperability:**

    6.1 Scaling Solutions for Layer-2: Scalability issues are resolved by putting layer-2 scaling techniques like state channels and sidechains into practice. By offloading certain transactions from the primary blockchain, these solutions guarantee more efficient tokenomic procedures during spikes in demand.

    6.2 Interoperability Protocols: Interoperability protocols are essential for reducing the dangers connected to ecosystem fragmentation. Initiatives can give top priority to integrating protocols such as the Interledger Protocol (ILP) and cross-chain bridges in order to enable smooth asset transfers between various blockchain networks, hence enhancing the tokenomic landscape's connectivity and usability.

7. **Reporting and Regulatory Compliance:**

    7.1 Internal Compliance Teams: Tokenomic projects have the option to set up internal compliance teams whose mission is to make sure that rules are followed. To maintain regulatory compliance, these teams can carry out routine evaluations, keep an eye on modifications to compliance standards, and make the required adjustments.

7.2 Transparency in Reporting: Gaining the confidence of regulators and users alike requires transparency in reporting. Projects ought to submit reports on a regular basis outlining the steps they have made to comply with regulations.

In addition to boosting user confidence, transparent reporting helps initiatives get favorable regulatory positioning.

7.3 Platforms for Regulatory Reporting: When regulatory reporting becomes commonplace, initiatives could think about using services or platforms that make compliance reporting easier and more efficient. These systems can offer templates, policies, and instruments to guarantee precise and effective reporting to regulatory bodies.

8. **International Engagement and Cooperation:**

8.1 Industry Collaboration: The development of uniform standards and best practices in the digital asset sector depends on industry collaboration. The sharing of knowledge, materials, and security procedures can be facilitated by industry groups, coalitions, or forums. Working together improves the group's ability to counter new threats.

8.2 International Engagement: International cooperation amongst regulatory authorities is essential given the global nature of digital assets. Working together can reduce the dangers of international fraud and hacking, make information sharing easier, and build unified standards that will make the ecosystem more uniform and safe for users and tokenomic initiatives.

8.3 Alliances & Partnerships: A collaborative approach to security is fostered by forming partnerships and alliances with other projects, industry stakeholders, and regulatory organizations. A strong and integrated tokenomic ecosystem is developed through pooled resources, insights, and cooperative efforts.

Chapter 7

FTT And The Global Economy

The idea of a Monetary Exchange Expense (FTT) has gotten momentum as a strategy device with the possibility to reshape the elements of monetary business sectors and add to income age for legislatures. FTT, otherwise called a Tobin charge, includes exacting a little expense on monetary exchanges, for example, stock exchanges and money trades. Defenders contend that FTT can control extreme theory, produce income for public money chests, and add to monetary solidness. Be that as it may, the execution of FTT likewise raises worries about its effect on market liquidity, monetary development, and worldwide seriousness. In this paper, we dive into the idea of FTT, looking at its verifiable setting, expected advantages, challenges, and the more extensive ramifications for the worldwide economy.

1. **Verifiable Setting of Monetary Exchange Duty:**
1. **Beginnings and Advancement:**
   Burdening monetary exchanges traces all the way back to the 1970s when Nobel laureate financial expert James Tobin proposed a duty on cash exchanges to check money hypothesis. Tobin's inspiration was to settle trade rates and forestall troublesome capital streams. While his unique proposition didn't build up some forward momentum, the idea of FTT has advanced throughout the long term.
   In ongoing many years, conversations around FTT have picked up speed as states look for creative ways of producing income and address worries about unnecessary gamble taking and market unpredictability. Various nations and districts have investigated varieties of FTT, each custom fitted to their particular monetary frameworks and financial needs.
2. **FTT in Various Wards:**

Sweden (1984-1991): Sweden carried out a protections exchange charge during the 1980s, regularly known as the Stockholm Trade Expense. The duty applied to buys and deals of protections on the Stockholm Stock Trade. Notwithstanding, the assessment was ultimately abrogated in 1991 because of worries about its effect on market seriousness and exchanging volumes.

Joined Realm (1986-2003): The Unified Realm carried out a stamp obligation on share exchanges in 1986, successfully going about as a type of FTT. The stamp obligation keeps on being set up, applying to the acquisition of offers on the London Stock Trade.

European Association (Proposed): The European Association has investigated the chance of carrying out a blended FTT across its part states. The proposed FTT plans to apply to a more extensive scope of monetary instruments, including stocks, bonds, and subordinates. Notwithstanding, dealings among part states have confronted difficulties, and the execution of the expansive FTT is yet to be understood.

Worldwide Backing: Supporters for FTT at the worldwide level contend that a planned exertion is expected to forestall tax avoidance and guarantee a level battleground for monetary business sectors around the world. Associations like the Unified Countries and the Worldwide Money related Asset have investigated the possible advantages and difficulties of a worldwide FTT.

II. Likely Advantages of Monetary Exchange Assessment:

1. **Income Age:**
   One of the essential inspirations driving carrying out FTT is the possibility to produce critical income for legislatures. The little expenses applied to each monetary exchange can gather into significant sums, giving another type of revenue for public uses. This income can be used for different purposes, including financing public administrations, foundation activities, and social projects.
2. **Checking Over the top Hypothesis:**
   FTT defenders contend that the expense can go about as a hindrance to inordinate hypothesis and momentary exchanging procedures. By forcing an expense on every exchange, FTT plans to deter high-recurrence exchanging and diminish market instability. This, thusly, could add to a more steady and strong monetary framework.
3. **Putting Dangerous Conduct down:**
   Monetary business sectors, on occasion, witness over the top gamble taking that can prompt market air pockets and crashes. FTT advocates fight that by adding an expense for exchanges, particularly those including complex monetary instruments, the duty can deter brokers from participating in excessively unsafe way of behaving. This might add to a more reasonable and stable monetary climate.
4. **Tending to Abundance Imbalance:**

FTT is much of the time outlined as an instrument for advancing more prominent monetary value by focusing on monetary exchanges basically embraced by richer people and institutional financial backers. The contention is that by forcing a duty on monetary exchanges, a part of the increases from monetary exercises would be diverted toward tending to cultural necessities, consequently adding to a more impartial dissemination of riches.

III. Difficulties and Reactions of Monetary Exchange Expense:

1. **Influence on Market Liquidity:**
   One of the essential worries raised against FTT is its likely effect on market liquidity. Pundits contend that the inconvenience of an expense on every exchange could prompt decreased exchanging volumes, making it more provoking for purchasers and merchants to track down counterparties. This decrease in liquidity might bring about more extensive bid-ask spreads and expanded exchange costs, especially for retail financial backers.
2. **Distortionary Impacts on Capital Streams:**
   FTT could prompt distortionary impacts on capital streams, particularly in a globalized monetary climate. Dealers might divert their exercises to locales without FTT, prompting a fracture of monetary business sectors. This could subvert the viability of FTT in accomplishing its planned objectives and result in unseen side-effects for the steadiness of the worldwide monetary framework.
3. **Likely Effect on Financial Development:**
   Pundits likewise contend that FTT can possibly hose financial development by forcing costs on capital arrangement and speculation. Higher exchange expenses might deter organizations from raising capital through the issuance of stocks and securities, restricting their capacity to subsidize development and advancement. This could have more extensive ramifications for work creation and generally speaking financial turn of events.
4. **Administrative Exchange:**

The worldwide idea of monetary business sectors considers administrative exchange, where market members might try to take advantage of contrasts in administrative systems across purviews. On the off chance that a few nations carry out FTT while others don't, there is a gamble that brokers will move their exercises to purviews without the expense, subverting the viability of FTT and making a lopsided battleground.

IV. Worldwide Economy: FTT and Global Coordination:

1. **The Requirement for Global Coordination:**
   The likely difficulties and reactions related with FTT highlight the significance of worldwide coordination. To address worries about market discontinuity and administrative exchange, a worldwide composed way to deal with FTT might be vital. Endeavors by associations, for example, the G20 or global bodies

like the Monetary Solidness Board could assume a pivotal part in encouraging coordinated effort among countries.

2. **Influence on Developing Business sectors:**
The execution of FTT in created economies could have suggestions for developing business sectors. As capital streams are diverted because of FTT, developing business sectors might encounter expanded unpredictability and difficulties in drawing in speculations. Facilitated endeavors to consider the particular requirements and conditions of arising economies would be fundamental to guarantee the solidness of the worldwide monetary framework.

3. **Adjusting Guideline and Advancement:**

FTT conversations ought to think about the sensitive harmony between controlling monetary business sectors and encouraging advancement. While FTT means to resolve issues connected with market overabundances, it shouldn't smother monetary development that assumes a critical part in driving financial development. Finding some kind of harmony requires cautious thought of the developing idea of monetary business sectors and mechanical progressions.

V. Future Patterns and Contemplations:

1. **Innovation and Authorization:**
Headways in monetary innovation (FinTech) may assume a part in the successful execution and requirement of FTT. Robotized frameworks and blockchain innovation can improve straightforwardness in monetary exchanges, making it simpler to track and collect the assessment. Legislatures and administrative bodies might have to use mechanical developments to guarantee the effective organization of FTT.

2. **Socially Mindful Money management:**
The developing pattern of socially mindful money management (SRI) may impact the talk around FTT. Financial backers progressively think about the cultural effect of their monetary exercises, and FTT lines up with the standards of dependable money by adding to public income and tending to abundance disparity. The reconciliation of SRI standards into monetary navigation might shape the acknowledgment of FTT in the speculation local area.

3. **Tending to Foundational Dangers:**

As conversations around FTT progress, there is a potential chance to address foundational gambles inside the monetary framework. Improved administrative systems, risk the executives rehearses, and an emphasis on monetary steadiness can supplement FTT measures. This all encompassing methodology is fundamental for building a versatile monetary engineering fit for enduring shocks and vulnerabilities.

7.1 FTT as a Catalyst for Economic Growth

The Monetary Exchange Expense (FTT), a proposed demand on different monetary exchanges, for example, stock exchanges and cash trades, has been a subject of extraordinary discussion in regards to its possible effect on the worldwide economy. While reactions have been raised, defenders contend that FTT, whenever carried out reasonably, can act as an impetus for financial development. This paper investigates the likely manners by which FTT can invigorate monetary development, analyzing its advantages, challenges, and the more extensive ramifications for monetary business sectors and government incomes.

1. **FTT and Income Age:**
1. **Financing Public Speculations:**
    One of the essential contentions for FTT is producing significant income for governments potential. The assets created from FTT can be diverted into public speculations, for example, foundation undertakings, schooling, and medical services. By giving extra assets to these basic regions, FTT can add to the establishment for supported financial development.
2. **Countering Monetary Imperatives:**

States frequently face monetary imperatives, particularly during financial slumps or emergencies. FTT offers an elective income stream that isn't dependent on conventional tax collection strategies. During seasons of financial strain, the income produced through FTT can be essential in keeping up with public administrations, supporting social projects, and balancing out the economy.

II. **FTT and Market Soundness:**

1. **Checking Unnecessary Theory:**
    FTT can possibly go about as an obstacle to unnecessary theory and transient exchanging. The burden of a little expense on each monetary exchange can deter high-recurrence exchanging methodologies, which frequently add to showcase unpredictability. By advancing a more steady exchanging climate, FTT can make an establishment for supportable financial development.
2. **Empowering Long haul Speculation:**

The drawn out strength of an economy is frequently intently attached to speculations that add to useful exercises. FTT, by beating transient speculative exchanging down, can divert market members towards additional long haul and vital ventures. This shift can prompt expanded capital arrangement, work creation, and by and large monetary turn of events.

III. **FTT and Monetary Value:**

1. **Tending to Abundance Imbalance:**
   FTT is regularly outlined as a device for advancing monetary value. By burdening monetary exchanges essentially embraced by more affluent people and institutional financial backers, FTT intends to address abundance disparity. The income produced can be utilized to finance projects and drives that benefit the more extensive populace, adding to a more evenhanded dissemination of assets.
2. **Boosting Comprehensive Financial Practices:**

The execution of FTT can empower a change in monetary practices towards more comprehensive and socially dependable way of behaving. Monetary organizations and financial backers might focus on ventures that line up with more extensive cultural objectives, realizing that a part of the returns will add to public government assistance. This arrangement of monetary exercises with social obligation can encourage a more maintainable and impartial financial climate.

IV. Difficulties and Relief Methodologies:

1. **Influence on Market Liquidity:**
   One of the essential worries related with FTT is its possible effect on market liquidity. Pundits contend that exchange expenses could prompt decreased exchanging volumes, making it more provoking for purchasers and dealers to execute exchanges. Moderation techniques could incorporate cautiously aligning the duty rate, giving exclusions to particular sorts of exchanges, or executing measures to help liquidity in impacted markets.
2. **Administrative Exchange:**
   The globalized idea of monetary business sectors raises worries about administrative exchange - the likelihood that brokers will move their exercises to purviews without FTT. To alleviate this gamble, global coordination is essential. A universally organized way to deal with FTT could forestall market discontinuity and guarantee a level battleground, limiting the potential for administrative exchange.
3. **Adjusting Monetary Development and Guideline:**

While FTT can possibly invigorate monetary development, finding some kind of harmony among guideline and cultivating innovation is fundamental. Policymakers ought to painstakingly consider the developing idea of monetary business sectors and mechanical headways to try not to smother financial development. This equilibrium might include carrying out FTT close by strong measures that energize mindful monetary development.

V. Worldwide Ramifications and Collaboration:

1. **Global Joint effort:**
   The fruitful execution of FTT and its viability as an impetus for monetary development rely upon global joint effort. Facilitated endeavors among countries can assist with tending to worries about administrative exchange, guaranteeing that FTT doesn't prompt market fracture or bends in capital streams. Worldwide bodies, for example, the G20 could assume a significant part in cultivating this coordinated effort.
2. **Contemplations for Developing Business sectors:**

The effect of FTT on developing business sectors requires cautious thought. As capital streams might be diverted because of the duty, arising economies might encounter expanded unpredictability and difficulties in drawing in ventures. Worldwide participation ought to consider the one of a kind conditions of developing business sectors to guarantee strength and inclusivity in the worldwide monetary framework.

VI. Future Patterns and Advancement:

1. **Mechanical Joining:**
   Progressions in monetary innovation (FinTech) could assume a crucial part in the effective execution of FTT. Mechanized frameworks and blockchain innovation can upgrade straightforwardness in monetary exchanges, making it simpler to follow and uphold the expense. Legislatures and administrative bodies ought to use mechanical advancements to guarantee the proficient organization of FTT.
2. **Socially Mindful Money management:**
   The developing pattern of socially capable financial planning (SRI) lines up with the standards of FTT. Financial backers progressively think about the cultural effect of their monetary exercises, and FTT adds to mindful money by tending to abundance imbalance and subsidizing public drives. The coordination of SRI standards into monetary navigation might shape the acknowledgment and viability of FTT.
3. **Developing Administrative Systems:**

As conversations around FTT progress, administrative systems should advance to adjust to changing business sector elements. Cooperation between state run administrations, administrative bodies, and monetary organizations is fundamental for plan viable and adaptable administrative systems that line up with the objectives of financial development, dependability, and social obligation.

7.2 International Adoption and Collaboration

Global reception and joint effort address fundamental features of an interconnected reality where countries, associations, and people cooperate to address shared difficulties, encourage common comprehension, and drive positive change. The trading of information, assets, and mastery on a worldwide scale is urgent in handling issues going from environmental change and general wellbeing to financial turn of events and civil rights. In this paper, we investigate the meaning of worldwide reception and cooperation, looking at the advantages, difficulties, and possible future headings of working all in all on a worldwide stage.

1. **The Significance of Global Reception:**
1. **Sharing Prescribed procedures:**
Global reception includes the dispersal and use of best practices across borders. As nations face normal difficulties, for example, general wellbeing emergencies or natural issues, the reception of fruitful procedures and arrangements starting with one area then onto the next can speed up progress. Gaining from one another's triumphs and disappointments cultivates an aggregate way to deal with critical thinking, guaranteeing that powerful techniques are carried out internationally.
2. **Innovation Move and Development:**
Worldwide reception stretches out past the sharing of thoughts; it incorporates the exchange of innovation and developments. Nations with cutting edge mechanical abilities can add to the advancement of less innovatively progressed districts, advancing financial development and worked on personal satisfaction. Joint effort in innovative work empowers the worldwide local area to bridle the capability of arising advances to serve humankind by and large.
3. **Limit Building and Instruction:**

By embracing global prescribed procedures and working together in training and limit building drives, countries can fortify their human resources. Preparing programs, trade projects, and associations between instructive organizations add to the improvement of gifted experts who can drive advancement and progress in different fields.

This cooperative methodology guarantees that information is shared, engaging people and networks to contribute genuinely to their social orders.

II. Cooperation in Tending to Worldwide Difficulties:

1. **Environmental Change Relief and Ecological Manageability:**
The test of environmental change requires a planned worldwide reaction. Global cooperation in creating and embracing reasonable practices, environmentally friendly power advancements, and preservation endeavors is fundamental. Arrangements, for example, the Paris Understanding represent the responsibility of countries to cooperate to decrease fossil fuel byproducts, safeguard biodiversity, and relieve the effects of environmental change on a planetary scale.
2. **General Wellbeing and Worldwide Pandemics:**
Worldwide wellbeing emergencies, like the Coronavirus pandemic, highlight the

significance of global cooperation in general wellbeing. The sharing of logical information, immunization circulation, and facilitated reaction endeavors are pivotal in controlling the spread of sicknesses that rise above borders. Cooperative drives like COVAX show the need of a brought together way to deal with address wellbeing challenges that influence networks around the world.

3. **Monetary Turn of events and Exchange:**

Global joint effort assumes a crucial part in advancing financial improvement through exchange and collaboration. Reciprocal and multilateral economic deals work with the trading of labor and products, encouraging monetary development and setting out open doors for countries to represent considerable authority in their areas of near advantage. Cooperative monetary drives, for example, the Belt and Street Drive, expect to improve foundation advancement and availability, driving worldwide financial advancement.

III. Challenges in Global Reception and Joint effort:

1. **Social Awareness and Variety:**
   One test in global reception and joint effort is exploring the assorted social scenes of partaking countries. Aversion to social contrasts, customs, and values is pivotal to guaranteeing that cooperative endeavors are conscious and comprehensive. Exploring these distinctions requires compelling correspondence, sympathy, and an eagerness to comprehend and consolidate different viewpoints.

2. **Power Elements and Disparity:**
   Power elements and existing disparities among countries can present difficulties to successful coordinated effort. A few nations might use more impact or have more prominent assets, possibly prompting irregular characteristics in direction and asset dispersion. Addressing these variations requires a guarantee to fair cooperation, where the interests and needs of all partaking parties are thought of and regarded.

3. **Political and International Difficulties:**

Political contemplations and international strains can block global coordinated effort. Conflicts among countries, changing political scenes, and verifiable struggles might obstruct the foundation of cooperative systems. Beating these difficulties requires political endeavors, global discourse, and a guarantee to figuring out some mutual interest for everyone's benefit.

IV. Examples of overcoming adversity in Global Reception and Joint effort:

1. **The Montreal Convention:**
   The Montreal Convention, a worldwide deal laid out in 1987, remains as an effective illustration of worldwide coordinated effort. Pointed toward safe-

guarding the ozone layer by transitioning away from the development of ozone-exhausting substances, the settlement has made huge progress. The joint effort among countries brought about the decrease of unsafe substances, showing the viability of global collaboration in tending to natural difficulties.

2. **Worldwide Antibody Drives:**
Worldwide immunization drives, like Gavi, the Antibody Partnership, and the Alliance for Scourge Readiness Advancements (CEPI), embody effective global cooperation in general wellbeing. These associations work to guarantee impartial admittance to immunizations, particularly in low-pay nations. The cooperative endeavors in creating and circulating Coronavirus immunizations feature the significance of an organized worldwide reaction to wellbeing emergencies.

3. **The European Association:**

The European Association (EU) is a striking illustration of monetary and political cooperation. Initially shaped to advance monetary participation, the EU has developed into a political and financial association. The single market, normal money (Euro), and shared establishments show the progress of cooperative endeavors in encouraging financial dependability, advancing exchange, and guaranteeing political collaboration among part states.

V. **Future Headings and Developments:**

1. **Advanced Availability and Virtual Coordinated effort:**
Progressions in computerized network offer new roads for global coordinated effort. Virtual coordinated effort stages, computerized specialized apparatuses, and remote work capacities empower people and associations to team up flawlessly across borders. The future might see an expanded dependence on advanced innovations to work with worldwide coordinated effort, making it more straightforward for different partners to cooperate regardless of actual distances.

2. **Practical Advancement Objectives (SDGs):**
The Unified Countries Practical Improvement Objectives (SDGs) give an exhaustive structure to worldwide cooperation. Countries all over the planet have focused on accomplishing these objectives, which incorporate targets connected with neediness easing, training, environment activity, and orientation fairness. As countries work all in all towards the SDGs, the structure fills in as a guide for cooperative endeavors in tending to worldwide difficulties.

3. **Cross-Sectoral Joint effort:**

The fate of global coordinated effort might include expanded cross-sectoral participation, uniting state run administrations, organizations, non-legislative associations (NGOs), and the scholarly community. Cooperative drives that range different areas can use assorted skill and assets to extensively address complex difficulties. Associations among public and confidential substances might turn out to be more predominant in driving advancement and supportable turn of events.

7.3 Implications for Developing Economies

Creating economies face a heap of difficulties and open doors in the steadily developing scene of the globalized world. While globalization has brought expanded interconnectedness and the potential for monetary development, it has additionally presented these economies to different dangers, weaknesses, and variations. In this exposition, we dive into the ramifications for creating economies, looking at the multilayered parts of globalization, and investigating procedures to explore difficulties and influence open doors for manageable turn of events.

1. **Globalization and Creating Economies:**
1. **Monetary Reconciliation and Exchange:**
    Globalization has altogether expanded monetary coordination, working with the development of merchandise, administrations, and capital across borders.
    For creating economies, this offers chances to take part in worldwide exchange, access bigger business sectors, and draw in unfamiliar speculations. In any case, the degree to which these advantages emerge relies upon the limit of these economies to take part actually in worldwide exchange organizations.
2. **Innovation Move and Advancement:**
    The exchange of innovation and developments across borders is a urgent part of globalization. Creating economies can profit from the reception of trend setting innovations that upgrade efficiency, proficiency, and intensity. In any case, challenges connected with mechanical framework, advanced education, and protected innovation freedoms can frustrate the full acknowledgment of these open doors.
3. **Capital Streams and Unfamiliar Direct Speculation (FDI):**

Globalization has worked with the progression of capital, including unfamiliar direct speculation (FDI), into creating economies. While FDI can acquire assets, aptitude, and open positions, it additionally raises worries about reliance, financial imbalance, and possible double-dealing. Adjusting the advantages and dangers of capital inflows is fundamental for creating economies to outfit the positive parts of globalization.

II. Challenges Looked by Creating Economies:

1. **Monetary Imbalance:**
    One of the critical difficulties looked by creating economies in the time of globalization is the compounding of monetary disparity. The advantages of globalization, like expanded exchange and unfamiliar speculation, frequently

lopsidedly favor specific sections of the populace or explicit districts inside a nation, prompting broadening pay holes.

2. **Weakness to Outside Shocks:**
Creating economies can be profoundly powerless against outside shocks, remembering monetary slumps for created nations, changes in ware costs, and worldwide monetary emergencies. These outside shocks can significantly affect the monetary soundness and development possibilities of agricultural countries, featuring the requirement for vigorous gamble the executives techniques.

3. **Ecological Supportability:**
The quest for monetary development in a globalized world has frequently come to the detriment of ecological maintainability. Creating economies might confront difficulties in adjusting the basic for industrialization and financial advancement with the need to address ecological debasement, environmental change, and asset consumption.

4. **Social and Social Interruptions:**

Globalization can achieve critical social and social changes in creating economies. The flood of unfamiliar societies, values, and ways of life might prompt social homogenization or, alternately, trigger obstruction and social pressures. Dealing with these elements requires cautious thought of the effect of globalization on nearby characters and social designs.

III. Amazing open doors for Creating Economies:

1. **Exchange Expansion and Market Access:**
Globalization offers creating economies the potential chance to differentiate their economies and access new business sectors. By growing their commodity base and partaking in provincial and worldwide economic deals, these countries can diminish reliance on a thin scope of items or exchanging accomplices, improving monetary versatility and manageability.

2. **Human Resources Improvement:**
Globalization puts an exceptional on human resources. Creating economies can exploit this pattern by putting resources into training, ability advancement, and medical care. A knowledgeable and gifted labor force improves the seriousness of these economies in the worldwide commercial center, drawing in speculations and encouraging development.

3. **Development and Business:**
Embracing development and business is basic for creating economies to flourish in a globalized climate. By cultivating a culture of advancement, putting resources into innovative work, and supporting enterprising endeavors, these countries can situate themselves as center points for imagination and mechanical progression.

4. **Maintainable Improvement Objectives (SDGs):**

The Unified Countries Maintainable Improvement Objectives (SDGs) give a complete system to creating economies to address social, monetary, and ecological difficulties. Adjusting public systems to the SDGs can direct these countries toward reasonable turn of events, guaranteeing that globalization adds to worked on expectations for everyday comforts, diminished imbalance, and natural preservation.

IV. Methodologies for Creating Economies:

1. **Comprehensive Monetary Approaches:**
   Creating economies should take on comprehensive financial arrangements that focus on impartial development and address pay variations. This includes executing measures to guarantee that the advantages of globalization are shared across various portions of the populace, diminishing neediness, and advancing social attachment.
2. **Building Strength to Outside Shocks:**
   To relieve weakness to outside shocks, creating economies need to fabricate strength in their financial designs. This incorporates differentiating kinds of revenue, putting resources into areas with stable interest, and laying out vigorous monetary frameworks that can endure worldwide financial variances.
3. **Reasonable Advancement Arranging:**
   Creating economies can coordinate manageability into their advancement arranging by taking on harmless to the ecosystem works on, putting resources into environmentally friendly power, and tending to asset the executives challenges. Adjusting public improvement procedures to worldwide supportability systems, like the SDGs, gives a guide to adjusted and economical development.
4. **Fortifying Organizations and Administration:**

Powerful administration and solid organizations are principal to exploring the difficulties of globalization. Creating economies ought to zero in on building straightforward, responsible, and responsive establishments that can oversee monetary coordination, direct unfamiliar speculation, and shield the interests of their residents.

V. Contextual analyses: Effective Systems in Creating Economies:

1. **Singapore:**
   Singapore, notwithstanding its little size and absence of normal assets, has turned into a worldwide financial force to be reckoned with. Through essential interests in schooling, foundation, and a favorable to business climate, Singapore has drawn in unfamiliar speculations and situated itself as a center for money, innovation, and exchange. The country's prosperity features the significance of visionary initiative and a promise to development.

2. **South Korea:**
   South Korea changed from a conflict attacked a financial juggernaut through an intentional spotlight on industrialization and innovative turn of events. The public authority assumed a urgent part in advancing key businesses, putting resources into training, and encouraging development.
   South Korea's story highlights the meaning of long haul arranging, government-industry cooperation, and a persistent quest for innovative progression.
3. **China:**

China's quick financial rising is a demonstration of the extraordinary force of globalization. By embracing market-situated changes, putting resources into framework, and turning into the "world's production line," China lifted millions out of destitution and turned into a central part in worldwide exchange. In any case, China's experience likewise brings up issues about ecological manageability, pay disparity, and the harmony between state control and market influences.

Chapter 8

Future Trends And Innovations

In a world that is continually developing, driven by progressions in innovation, changes in cultural designs, and the ascent of worldwide difficulties, what's to come is set apart by a determined quest for development. As we stand at the intersection of uncommon change, understanding and expecting future patterns become urgent for exploring the way forward. This exposition investigates the multi-layered scene of future patterns and developments, traversing different spaces like innovation, medical care, maintainability, instruction, and cultural effects. By diving into these arising patterns, we plan to acquire experiences into the groundbreaking powers that will shape our aggregate future and the significant effect they will have on social orders around the world.

1. **Presentation**

The speed of development has gone through a seismic shift over the entire course of time, with every period set apart by unmistakable mechanical headways and cultural changes. The speed increase of development is a principal quality of the contemporary scene, driven by a blend of variables like quick innovative advancement, expanded network, and the globalization of data. As we explore the intricacies representing things to come, grasping the exchange of these elements and their suggestions for the direction of innovation is fundamental.

1. **The Speed increase of Development**

To contextualize the present status of development, pondering the verifiable movement of mechanical advancements is important. From the modern upset to the data age, every time has achieved groundbreaking changes that have reshaped the texture of social orders. The speed increase of development in ongoing many years can be credited to a conjunction of variables, remembering progressions for processing power, the coming of the web, and the democratization of

information. Understanding the verifiable setting permits us to see the value in the fast speed at which development is happening and gives an establishment to foreseeing future patterns.
2. **The Interconnected Future**

One of the central traits representing things to come is the rising interconnectivity of different mechanical spaces. The union of advances, frequently alluded to as the Fourth Modern Unrest, includes the coordination of man-made consciousness (simulated intelligence), web of things (IoT), blockchain, and other state of the art innovations. This transaction sets out cooperative energies and open doors for advancement that stretch out past the limits of individual disciplines. The ascent of interdisciplinary cooperation becomes principal in this interconnected future, as forward leaps are progressively the aftereffect of cooperative endeavors that draw on ability from different fields.

II. Innovation: Molding the Advanced Boondocks

1. **Man-made consciousness and AI**
   The cutting edge of mechanical development is overwhelmed by man-made brainpower (computer based intelligence) and AI (ML). Progressions in artificial intelligence calculations, energized by the accessibility of immense datasets and strong processing assets, have prompted noteworthy leap forwards. AI applications penetrate different businesses, from medical care and money to assembling and amusement. Be that as it may, the expansion of man-made intelligence raises moral worries, inciting conversations about mindful artificial intelligence advancement, straightforwardness, and the expected effect on business.
2. **Quantum Registering**
   As traditional figuring approaches its limits, the field of quantum registering arises as a troublesome power. Quantum PCs influence the standards of quantum mechanics to perform complex estimations at speeds unbelievable by traditional PCs. Leap forwards in quantum registering research are turning out to be more regular, with organizations and examination establishments overall dashing to accomplish quantum matchless quality. The viable utilizations of quantum figuring stretch out to cryptography, enhancement issues, and reenactments with expansive results.
3. **Web of Things (IoT)**
   The expansion of associated gadgets, all in all known as the Web of Things (IoT), is changing the manner in which we collaborate with the world. From brilliant homes and wearables to modern sensors and shrewd urban areas, the IoT environment is growing quickly. The information created by interconnected gadgets offer significant bits of knowledge for organizations, legislatures, and people. Be

that as it may, the rising predominance of IoT gadgets additionally raises worries about protection, security, and the potential for pernicious abuse.

4. Increased and Computer generated Reality

Increased reality (AR) and augmented reality (VR) advancements are reshaping the scene of amusement, gaming, schooling, and different enterprises. AR improves this present reality climate with computerized overlays, while VR submerges clients in a reproduced climate. The uses of AR and VR stretch out past diversion, with instructive organizations utilizing these advancements for vivid opportunities for growth, and medical care experts using them for preparing and recreation.

III. Medical care: Changing Wellbeing

1. **Accuracy Medication**
Progressions in genomics and customized medication are introducing a time of accuracy medication. Fitting clinical medicines in light of a person's hereditary cosmetics considers more viable and designated mediations. The incorporation of genomic information into medical care rehearses presents additional opportunities for illness counteraction, finding, and therapy. In any case, the moral contemplations encompassing hereditary protection and the potential for segregation require cautious route.

2. **Telemedicine**
The computerized change of medical care is exemplified by the ascent of telemedicine. Virtual meetings, distant patient checking, and computerized wellbeing stages are becoming essential parts of current medical care frameworks. The comfort of telemedicine further develops admittance to medical care administrations, especially in remote or underserved regions. As the limits among physical and advanced medical care obscure, the moral ramifications of far off medical care conveyance and information security come to the front line.

3. **Biotechnology and Quality Altering**
Progressions in biotechnology, especially CRISPR-based quality altering, can possibly reform the treatment of hereditary issues. The capacity to alter the human genome brings up moral issues about the restrictions of mediation and the outcomes of messing with the basic structure blocks of life. The continuous exchange encompassing the capable utilization of quality altering advances mirrors the fragile harmony between logical advancement and moral contemplations.

4. **Wellbeing Tech and Wearables**

The combination of innovation into medical care stretches out past the clinical setting, with the multiplication of wellbeing tech gadgets and wearables. These gadgets, going from wellness trackers to smartwatches with wellbeing checking abilities, engage people to assume responsibility for their prosperity.

The information gathered by these gadgets add to a more all encompassing way to deal with medical services, stressing preventive measures and proactive wellbeing the board.

IV. Manageability: Graphing a Green Future

1. **Environmentally friendly power**
   The basic to address environmental change is driving headways in sustainable power advances. Sun based and wind power, specifically, have seen critical leap forwards, making them progressively feasible options in contrast to conventional non-renewable energy sources. The progress to a perfect energy economy isn't just an ecological need yet in addition a monetary open door, with environmentally friendly power sources offering economical answers for satisfying developing worldwide energy needs.
2. **Roundabout Economy**
   The idea of a roundabout economy challenges the customary direct model of creation and utilization. Underlining the decrease of waste and the reuse of assets, a roundabout economy plans to make a regenerative framework. Developments in reusing advances, feasible item plan, and waste administration add to the vision of a round economy, where materials are persistently cycled, limiting ecological effect.
3. **Maintainable Agribusiness**
   The crossing point of innovation and agribusiness, known as accuracy cultivating, is changing the manner in which we produce food. From accuracy water system frameworks to sensor-prepared farm vehicles, innovation is upgrading agrarian practices for effectiveness and supportability. The quest for maintainable horticulture reaches out to hereditary designing for crop flexibility, as well as the improvement of elective protein sources to address the ecological difficulties related with conventional animals cultivating.
4. **Green Transportation**

The transportation area is a critical supporter of fossil fuel byproducts, making developments in green transportation significant for relieving the effect of environmental change. Electric vehicles (EVs), controlled by environmentally friendly power sources, are getting momentum as a manageable option in contrast to conventional petroleum product fueled vehicles. Also, headways in open transportation, including high velocity rail and metropolitan portability arrangements, add to making harmless to the ecosystem and productive transportation frameworks.

V. Training: Changing the Learning Scene

1. **Web based Learning and Far off Schooling**
   The computerized change reaches out to the domain of schooling, with web

based learning stages and distant instruction turning out to be progressively common. The openness of instructive assets, combined with the adaptability of web based learning, has democratized schooling on a worldwide scale. Virtual homerooms and cooperative internet based apparatuses are reshaping customary instruction models, permitting students to draw in with instructive substance paying little heed to geological imperatives.
2. **Computerized reasoning in Schooling**
Computerized reasoning is making critical advances into instruction, offering customized growth opportunities and inventive educating apparatuses. Computer based intelligence calculations examine individual learning styles, adjusting instructive substance to suit the requirements of every understudy. While the expected advantages of computer based intelligence in training are significant, moral worries connected with information security, algorithmic predisposition, and the job of human teachers in the growing experience should be painstakingly thought of.
3. **Deep rooted Learning**

The idea of deep rooted learning is acquiring unmistakable quality notwithstanding quickly developing position markets and innovative progressions. Nonstop expertise advancement and the capacity to adjust to new innovations are becoming fundamental for profession flexibility. Deep rooted learning drives, upheld by online courses, proficient advancement programs, and upskilling valuable open doors, enable people to remain important in an always evolving scene.

VI. Cultural Effects: Exploring Change

1. **The Fate of Work**
The coordination of robotization, simulated intelligence, and advanced mechanics into different ventures is reshaping the scene of business. While computerization can possibly upgrade proficiency and efficiency, it likewise raises worries about work uprooting and the requirement for reskilling. The fate of work is described by a shift towards more adaptable work game plans, far off business, and the rise of the gig economy.
2. **Moral Contemplations in Innovation**
As innovation turns into an indispensable piece of day to day existence, moral contemplations become the dominant focal point. Issues like information security, algorithmic predisposition, and the cultural effect of arising advancements require smart thought. Finding some kind of harmony between mechanical advancement and moral standards is fundamental to guarantee that development serves everyone's benefit without compromising basic qualities.
3. **Social and Social Movements**

The unavoidable impact of innovation on friendly and social standards is obvious in the manner we convey, consume data, and associate with the world. The ascent of virtual entertainment, for instance, has changed the elements of correspondence and local area commitment. Social movements achieved by mechanical advancements brief reflections on character, security, and the idea of human associations.

8.1 Evolving Landscape of Tokenomics

The idea of tokenomics, the financial model overseeing the creation, dispersion, and use of tokens, has gone through a significant change as of late. Starting from the universe of digital forms of money, tokenomics has extended past its underlying extension to turn into an essential part of different blockchain-based environments. This exposition investigates the developing scene of tokenomics, diving into its verifiable setting, the key parts molding its advancement, and the ramifications for the more extensive monetary and innovative scenes.

1. **Verifiable Setting:**
1. **Development of Tokenomics in Cryptographic forms of money**
   Tokenomics originally acquired unmistakable quality with the coming of Bitcoin, the spearheading digital currency presented in 2009. Bitcoin's decentralized nature and restricted supply set up for the investigation of monetary models inside advanced resources. Notwithstanding, it was the presentation of Ethereum in 2015 that really prepared for the advancement of tokenomics. Ethereum's savvy contract capacities empowered the making of different tokens, establishing the groundwork for the more extensive symbolic economy.
2. **Starting Coin Contributions (ICOs) and Token Deals**

The underlying flood in tokenomics development accompanied the ascent of Beginning Coin Contributions (ICOs) around 2017. ICOs gave a raising money instrument to blockchain projects, permitting them to circulate utility tokens to financial backers. This undeniable a takeoff from conventional funding subsidizing and democratized admittance to venture valuable open doors.

Nonetheless, the absence of administrative oversight prompted worries about misrepresentation and the requirement for more practical tokenomics models.

II. **Key Parts of Advancing Tokenomics:**

1. **Token Utility and Usefulness**
   The development of tokenomics is unpredictably connected to the utility and usefulness of tokens inside a given biological system. While early digital currencies principally filled in for the purpose of trade, current tokens frequently have diverse utility, going from administration and marking to empowering admittance to explicit elements inside decentralized applications (DApps). The

flexibility of tokens adds to the powerful idea of contemporary tokenomics models.

2. **Decentralized Money (DeFi) and Yield Cultivating**

   Decentralized Money (DeFi) has arisen as an extraordinary power inside the digital currency space, reshaping conventional monetary administrations through blockchain innovation. DeFi stages influence tokenomics to make decentralized loaning, acquiring, and exchanging environments. Yield cultivating, a training where clients give liquidity to decentralized trades in return for yield-bearing tokens, embodies the imaginative manners by which tokenomics is used to boost client support.

3. **Non-Fungible Tokens (NFTs)**

   Non-fungible tokens (NFTs) have acquainted another aspect with tokenomics, underscoring advanced proprietorship and uniqueness. NFTs address interesting computerized or actual resources on blockchain stages, empowering makers to tokenize and adapt advanced craftsmanship, collectibles, and, surprisingly, land. The shortage and credibility of NFTs add to their worth, and their development has differentiated the utilization instances of tokenomics past conventional monetary applications.

4. **Administration Tokens and DAOs**

Administration tokens assume a critical part in decentralized independent associations (DAOs), empowering token holders to take part in dynamic cycles. Token-based administration models engage networks to guide the turn of events and heading of decentralized projects aggregately. This majority rule way to deal with administration challenges customary progressive designs, giving a brief look into the likely fate of hierarchical direction.

III. Suggestions for the Monetary Scene:

1. **Democratization of Money**

   One of the huge ramifications of developing tokenomics is the democratization of money. Decentralized stages, worked with by tokenomics models, empower more extensive admittance to monetary administrations. Clients overall can partake in loaning, acquiring, exchanging, and contributing without depending on customary monetary mediators. This shift difficulties conventional power designs and encourages monetary incorporation on a worldwide scale.

2. **Challenges and Administrative Contemplations**

   While the democratization of money is a promising part of developing tokenomics, it likewise presents difficulties. Administrative systems linger behind the fast speed of advancement in the blockchain space, prompting vulnerabilities and possible dangers for financial backers. Finding some kind of harmony between cultivating development and safeguarding market members is a key test that controllers overall are wrestling with as they try to adjust to the changing scene of tokenomics.

3. **Combination with Customary Money**

The development of tokenomics isn't happening in separation; rather, it is bit by bit coordinating with conventional money. The idea of tokenized resources, where certifiable resources are addressed on blockchain stages, is getting some decent forward movement. This convergence of customary money and tokenomics can possibly overcome any issues between heritage monetary frameworks and the decentralized future imagined by blockchain aficionados.

IV. Innovative Progressions and Interoperability:

1. **Blockchain Interoperability**
As the quantity of blockchain organizations and stages keeps on developing, the significance of interoperability turns out to be progressively obvious. Endeavors to empower consistent correspondence and worth exchange between divergent blockchain networks add to the development of tokenomics. Interoperability permits clients to use the qualities of various blockchains, cultivating joint effort and extending the potential outcomes of token-based biological systems.

2. **Savvy Agreement Overhauls and Guidelines**

The programmable idea of savvy contracts empowers constant redesigns and the execution of new symbolic principles. Ethereum's change to Ethereum 2.0, with its move from a proof-of-work to a proof-of-stake agreement component, represents the flexibility of blockchain innovation.

New symbolic norms, for example, ERC-20 and ERC-721, present upgrades in usefulness and security, further molding the scene of tokenomics.

V. Future Patterns and Developments:

1. **National Bank Computerized Monetary forms (CBDCs)**
The development of National Bank Computerized Monetary forms (CBDCs) addresses a change in perspective in the worldwide monetary scene. While not rigorously sticking to the decentralized ethos of cryptographic forms of money, CBDCs integrate components of tokenomics to digitize public monetary standards. The mix of CBDCs into the current monetary foundation could overcome any barrier between customary government issued types of money and the computerized resource environment.

2. **Maintainability and Green Tokenomics**
The natural effect of blockchain networks, especially those utilizing evidence of-work agreement instruments, has gone under examination. Advancements in green tokenomics expect to address these worries by growing more energy-

proficient agreement components or changing to harmless to the ecosystem choices. Supportability contemplations are becoming essential to the development of tokenomics, mirroring a more extensive cultural shift towards eco-accommodating practices.

3. **Coordination of Man-made brainpower (artificial intelligence) with Tokenomics**

The convergence of tokenomics and man-made brainpower presents energizing opportunities for what's in store. Man-made intelligence calculations can be utilized to improve tokenomics models, upgrade safety efforts, and anticipate market patterns. The cooperative energy among simulated intelligence and tokenomics may prompt more proficient decentralized frameworks, computerized administration processes, and further developed risk the board inside blockchain biological systems.

8.2 Integration with Emerging Technologies (AI, IoT, etc.)

The fast speed of mechanical progression has led to a scene where coordination with arising innovations isn't simply a pattern however an essential goal. Organizations, ventures, and social orders are bridling the force of mix to open additional opportunities, smooth out tasks, and encourage advancement. In this exposition, we dive into the reconciliation of blockchain with other arising advances, like Man-made consciousness (man-made intelligence), the Web of Things (IoT), and that's just the beginning. Inspecting these cooperative energies gives experiences into the groundbreaking capability of cooperative advances and their effect on different areas.

1. **Blockchain and Man-made reasoning (computer based intelligence):**
1. **Collaborations in Information The board**

    The mix of blockchain and artificial intelligence is reshaping the scene of information the board. Blockchain's decentralized and secure record framework guarantees straightforwardness and changelessness, relieving concerns connected with information honesty. When joined with computer based intelligence, which succeeds in information examination and example acknowledgment, associations can get significant bits of knowledge from tremendous datasets put away on blockchain networks. This collaboration improves the exactness and dependability of computer based intelligence driven dynamic cycles.

2. **Decentralized AI**

    Blockchain's decentralized nature adjusts consistently with the standards of AI. Decentralized AI (DML) models influence the conveyed idea of blockchain organizations to prepare calculations without the requirement for a concentrated power. This upgrades information security as well as empowers cooperative advancing across dissimilar datasets. The joining of blockchain and man-made intelligence in DML is especially important in businesses where information responsiveness and security are principal, like medical services and money.

3. Shrewd Agreements Improving Computerization

Shrewd agreements, self-executing contracts with the particulars of the understanding straightforwardly composed into code, are a major part of blockchain innovation. When coordinated with man-made intelligence, brilliant agreements gain the ability to adjust in light of ongoing information powerfully. This empowers the mechanization of perplexing business processes, decreasing the requirement for go-betweens and speeding up the execution of legally binding commitments. The cooperative energy among blockchain and computer based intelligence driven savvy contracts can possibly change ventures, upgrading productivity and lessening functional expenses.

II. Blockchain and the Web of Things (IoT):

1. **Decentralized IoT Engineering**
   The Web of Things (IoT) includes the interconnectedness of gadgets, sensors, and frameworks to gather and trade information. Blockchain's decentralized engineering improves the security and uprightness of IoT organizations. By circulating information across hubs in the organization, blockchain limits the gamble of a weak link or malignant altering. This is especially vital in applications where the unwavering quality and security of information, like in brilliant urban communities or modern IoT, are central.
2. **Upgraded Security and Confidence in IoT**
   Blockchain's innate security highlights, for example, cryptographic encryption and agreement components, reinforce the reliability of information created by IoT gadgets. Safely recording and confirming the provenance of information on a blockchain guarantees that the data sent between IoT gadgets is precise and has not been messed with. This joining tends to online protection concerns and imparts trust in the unwavering quality of IoT organizations.
3. **Smoothing out Production network The board**

The coordination of blockchain and IoT is reforming inventory network the executives by giving start to finish perceivability and straightforwardness. IoT gadgets outfitted with sensors can transfer constant information on the area, condition, and status of merchandise. This information is safely recorded on a blockchain, making an unchanging record open to all partners. The outcome is a productive and straightforward store network environment, lessening shortcomings, limiting extortion, and upgrading discernibility.

III. Blockchain and Expanded Reality (AR)/Computer generated Reality (VR):

1. **Upgrading Vivid Encounters**
   The blend of blockchain and Expanded Reality (AR) or Augmented Reality

(VR) makes vivid and secure encounters. Blockchain's part in confirming and getting computerized resources lines up with the requirements of AR and VR applications. For example, blockchain can be utilized to validate virtual resources in gaming or confirm the legitimacy of computerized workmanship in virtual displays. This joining guarantees that virtual encounters are outwardly convincing as well as upheld by a safe and straightforward framework.

2. **Tokenization of Virtual Resources**

Blockchain's tokenization abilities find collaboration with AR and VR by empowering the making of computerized tokens addressing virtual resources. Whether it's virtual land, in-game things, or computerized collectibles, these tokens can be safely put away on a blockchain, giving clients genuine proprietorship and working with consistent exchanges across virtual conditions. This incorporation opens new adaptation models and monetary biological systems inside virtual spaces.

IV. Blockchain and Edge Processing:

1. **Conveying Processing Assets**

   Edge figuring, which includes handling information nearer to the wellspring of information age, lines up with the decentralized idea of blockchain.

   Incorporating blockchain with edge figuring considers the dispersion of registering assets across an organization of hubs. This guarantees that computational errands are effectively overseen at the edge, lessening inactivity and improving the general execution of decentralized applications (DApps).

2. **Getting Edge Gadgets**

Security is a vital worry in edge figuring, particularly as gadgets at the edge of an organization are more powerless to digital dangers. Blockchain's cryptographic conventions and decentralized agreement systems add to getting edge gadgets. Every exchange or information move can be safely recorded on the blockchain, lessening the gamble of unapproved access and guaranteeing the honesty of information at the edge.

V. Blockchain and Quantum Figuring:

1. **Tending to Quantum Dangers**

   The appearance of quantum figuring represents a possible danger to the cryptographic calculations that as of now secure blockchain networks. To address this test, specialists are investigating the joining of blockchain with post-quantum cryptography. By integrating quantum-safe cryptographic procedures, blockchain organizations can plan for the future scene where quantum PCs might represent a danger to customary encryption techniques.

2. **Quantum-Secure Blockchain Organizations**

The reconciliation of blockchain and quantum processing stretches out past tending to security concerns. Quantum PCs themselves can be utilized inside blockchain organizations to proficiently play out particular sorts of calculations more. Quantum-safe calculations can be carried out inside brilliant agreements, guaranteeing that blockchain networks stay secure even in the time of quantum registering.

VI. Difficulties and Contemplations:

1. **Adaptability and Execution**
   Regardless of the promising cooperative energies, incorporating blockchain with arising advances presents versatility and execution challenges. Blockchain organizations, especially those utilizing confirmation of-work agreement components, may confront limits in taking care of an enormous number of exchanges each second. Adaptability arrangements, like layer-two conventions and sharding, are being investigated to improve the exhibition of blockchain networks.
2. **Administrative Structures**
   The advancing scene of incorporated advancements delivers administrative difficulties. As these innovations cross, questions in regards to purview, information protection, and administrative consistence become complicated. State run administrations and administrative bodies are attempting to lay out systems that balance the requirement for development with the need of shopper assurance and information security.
3. **Interoperability**

Guaranteeing consistent interoperability between dissimilar blockchain networks and arising innovations stays a huge test. Endeavors to make principles and conventions that empower various advancements to convey actually are progressing. Accomplishing interoperability is urgent for understanding the maximum capacity of coordinated advancements in making exhaustive, interconnected biological systems.

VII. Future Headings and Developments:

1. **Cross-Chain Interoperability**
   The eventual fate of coordinated advancements lies in accomplishing consistent interoperability between various blockchain networks. Cross-chain arrangements, like interoperability conventions and scaffolds, are being created to empower the exchange of resources and information across divergent blockchain biological systems. This development is fundamental for making a strong and interconnected blockchain scene.
2. **Independent and Self-Overseeing Frameworks**
   As blockchain coordinates with artificial intelligence and savvy contracts become more refined, the development of independent and self-administering frameworks is not too far off. These frameworks, represented by predefined

rules and man-made intelligence driven dynamic cycles, can possibly improve asset assignment, upgrade security, and smooth out complex activities without the requirement for human mediation.

3. **Tokenization Past Computerized Resources**

The idea of tokenization is developing past advanced resources and digital forms of money. Coordinating blockchain with arising advances will prompt the tokenization of true resources, licensed innovation, and, surprisingly, individual information. This shift can possibly democratize admittance to different types of significant worth and rethink conventional ideas of possession.

8.3 Predictions for the Next Decade

As we stand at the cliff of another ten years, the expectation of mechanical, cultural, and worldwide changes is tangible. Anticipating what's in store is innately difficult, yet looking at latest things, mechanical progressions, and cultural movements gives important bits of knowledge into the likely directions of the following decade. In this paper, we investigate expectations for the approaching ten years across different spaces, including innovation, medical care, environmental change, international affairs, and cultural movements, offering a brief look into the developing scene that will shape our aggregate future.

1. **Innovation: The Speed increase of Advancement**
1. **Computerized reasoning and AI**

    The following ten years is ready to observe a quantum jump in the capacities of computerized reasoning (computer based intelligence) and AI (ML). As computational power increments and datasets become greater, computer based intelligence calculations will turn out to be more refined, empowering leap forwards in regular language handling, PC vision, and complex critical thinking. We can expect simulated intelligence turning out to be progressively coordinated into different parts of our regular routines, from customized remote helpers to computer based intelligence driven dynamic in business and medical care.

2. **Quantum Figuring**

    Quantum figuring, presently in its earliest stages, is supposed to develop fundamentally throughout the following 10 years. As specialists defeat specialized difficulties and foster versatile quantum frameworks, we might see reasonable applications arise in regions like cryptography, drug disclosure, advancement issues, and environment displaying. Quantum PCs can possibly upset enterprises by taking care of intricate issues at speeds right now incomprehensible with traditional registering.

3. **Increased Reality (AR) and Computer generated Reality (VR)**

    The following ten years will probably see an inescapable mix of increased and computer generated reality into our everyday encounters. AR and VR advances will reach out past amusement and gaming, tracking down applications in training, medical services, distant cooperation, and even customer retail. The advancement of more vivid and intuitive AR/VR encounters will reshape how we learn, work, and communicate with data.

4. **Network: 5G and Then some**

The worldwide rollout of 5G organizations is now in progress, however the following ten years will observer its broad reception and the investigation of considerably quicker, more solid correspondence advancements. Past 5G, progressions in remote correspondence, for example, 6G, could open additional opportunities, empowering continuous network for an undeniably interconnected world. This could prompt developments in IoT, savvy urban communities, and the consistent reconciliation of gadgets into our day to day routines.

II. **Medical care: Customized Medication and Mechanical Headways**

1. **Accuracy Medication**
   The following ten years holds gigantic commitment for the field of medical care, with a shift towards customized and accuracy medication. Progresses in genomics, information examination, and man-made intelligence will empower medical care experts to tailor therapy plans in view of a person's hereditary cosmetics, way of life, and explicit wellbeing needs. This shift from one-size-fits-all ways to deal with customized mediations could alter illness avoidance, conclusion, and treatment.
2. **Telemedicine and Far off Medical care**
   The sped up reception of telemedicine during the Coronavirus pandemic is probably going to persevere and extend over the course of the following 10 years. Improved telehealth stages, wearable gadgets, and distant patient checking advancements will upgrade the openness of medical care administrations. The accommodation of virtual counsels will engage people to deal with their wellbeing proactively, decreasing the weight on conventional medical care frameworks.
3. **Bioengineering and Quality Treatment**

Bioengineering and quality treatment are ready to upset the therapy of hereditary problems and constant infections. CRISPR and other quality altering advancements will turn out to be more refined, possibly offering solutions for already untreatable circumstances. Moral contemplations encompassing quality altering will keep on being a point of convergence of conversations, and administrative systems will develop to explore the intricacies of controlling the human genome.

III. **Environmental Change: Embracing Maintainability**

1. **Environmentally friendly power Progress**
   The following ten years will observer a critical speed increase in the progress towards sustainable power sources. Propels in sun based, wind, and other clean energy advances will drive down costs, making them more financially practical than petroleum derivatives.
   Legislatures, organizations, and networks overall will progressively embrace economical energy arrangements, with an emphasis on lessening fossil fuel by-products and moderating the effects of environmental change.
2. **Roundabout Economy Practices**
   The idea of a roundabout economy, underlining waste decrease, reusing, and reusing, will acquire noticeable quality. Organizations will embrace round practices to limit natural effect and advance reasonable utilization. Imaginative ways to deal with squander the board and item configuration will arise, changing ventures and decreasing dependence on limited assets.
3. **Green Transportation**

The auto business is on the cusp of a green transformation, with electric vehicles (EVs) set to turn out to be more standard. Progresses in battery innovation, expanded charging framework, and government motivations will add to the far and wide reception of EVs. Furthermore, advancements in manageable metropolitan transportation, for example, high velocity rail and independent electric vehicles, will shape the eventual fate of portability.

IV. International affairs: Moving Power Elements

1. **Innovation and Financial Authority**
   The following ten years is probably going to observe further changes in worldwide financial authority, driven to some extent by mechanical headways. Countries at the front line of development in computer based intelligence, quantum registering, and other state of the art innovations will fundamentally affect the worldwide financial scene. The opposition for mechanical matchless quality might reshape international partnerships and power structures.
2. **Network protection Difficulties**
   As innovation turns out to be more necessary to day to day existence and basic foundation, the significance of online protection will raise. The following ten years will probably see an expansion in digital dangers, with state-supported assaults, ransomware, and information breaks turning out to be more complex. Countries and associations will put vigorously in network protection measures, and worldwide collaboration will be critical in tending to worldwide digital dangers.
3. **Environment Tact and Worldwide Participation**

The earnestness of tending to environmental change will require upgraded global participation and discretion. The following ten years will see a developing accentuation on multilateral endeavors to battle natural difficulties.

Environment arrangements, practical improvement objectives, and cooperative drives will become urgent instruments in exploring the complicated exchange between natural manageability and international soundness.

V. Cultural Movements: Reshaping Work, Schooling, and Social Elements

1. **The Eventual fate of Work**
   The idea of work is going through a change in outlook, with remote work, gig economy cooperation, and adaptable game plans turning out to be more common. Robotization and simulated intelligence reception will change work jobs, requiring an emphasis on reskilling and upskilling. The following ten years will see a reexamination of conventional work structures, as organizations adjust to a more unique and innovation driven business scene.
2. **Deep rooted Learning and Nonstop Training**
   The accentuation on ceaseless acquiring and expertise improvement will escalate in the following ten years. The fast speed of innovative change will expect people to embrace long lasting learning, with an emphasis on getting versatile abilities. Online training stages, proficient improvement programs, and creative learning strategies will enable people to explore advancing vocation scenes.
3. **Social Elements and Computerized Network**

The effect of computerized network on friendly elements will keep on developing. Online entertainment, increased reality, and augmented reality will reshape how people associate, convey, and share encounters. The limits among physical and advanced real factors will obscure, introducing the two amazing open doors and difficulties for encouraging significant associations in an undeniably computerized world.

Chapter 9

Challenges And Opportunities For Investors

Putting resources into the present unique worldwide market presents a plenty of difficulties and open doors for financial backers. The scene is set apart by quick innovative progressions, international vulnerabilities, and the continuous effect of worldwide occasions, for example, pandemics and environmental change. In this exposition, we investigate the diverse parts of financial planning, analyzing the difficulties financial backers face and the open doors that emerge in exploring the intricacies of the contemporary speculation climate.

1. **Challenges for Financial backers:**
1. **International Vulnerabilities:**
   Exchange Strains and Duties: International pressures, especially exchange debates and levy clashes between significant economies, can disturb worldwide stock chains and effect the productivity of global organizations. Financial backers need to screen international turns of events and survey the likely effect on their venture portfolios.
   Worldwide Contentions and Shakiness: Political struggles and international flimsiness in different areas can make vulnerabilities for financial backers. Occasions like equipped struggles, sanctions, or political emergencies can prompt market instability and effect the exhibition of explicit enterprises or areas.
2. **Financial Instability:**
   Market Variances: Financial backers frequently face difficulties related with market vacillations. Monetary markers, loan fee changes, and unanticipated occasions can set off cost unpredictability, making it urgent for financial backers to utilize risk the board methodologies to safeguard their portfolios.
   Expansion and Collapse Concerns: Expansion and flattening can essentially affect venture returns. Financial backers should explore the sensitive harmony between protecting capital in the midst of expansion and looking for returns that dominate deflationary tensions.

3. **Innovative Interruptions:**
   Fast Mechanical Changes: The speed of innovative development presents the two valuable open doors and difficulties. Ventures going through quick mechanical changes can deliver existing plans of action outdated, influencing the presentation of customary speculations. Financial backers need to recognize drifts and adjust to the advancing innovative scene.
   Network safety Dangers: With expanding dependence on advanced foundation, financial backers face online protection gambles. Cyberattacks on organizations can bring about monetary misfortunes and reputational harm. Assessing the network safety proportions of potential ventures is pivotal for shielding portfolios.
4. **Natural, Social, and Administration (ESG) Elements:**
   Environmental Change Concerns: The developing familiarity with environmental change and its effect on organizations has prompted an emphasis on maintainable money management. Financial backers need to consider ecological dangers and the versatility of organizations despite environment related difficulties.
   Social and Administration Issues: Financial backers are progressively considering social and administration factors in their direction. Issues, for example, corporate administration practices, variety and consideration, and social obligation can influence the drawn out manageability of speculations.
5. **Administrative Changes:**

Worldwide Administrative Scene: Financial backers face difficulties connected with the always advancing worldwide administrative climate. Changes in guidelines, charge approaches, or economic deals can significantly affect venture procedures and require consistent checking.
   Consistence and Detailing Necessities: Consistence with administrative prerequisites and announcing guidelines presents difficulties for financial backers. Remaining informed about changes in detailing principles and guaranteeing adherence to consistence measures is fundamental to stay away from legitimate and monetary dangers.

II. **Valuable open doors for Financial backers:**

1. **Innovative Progressions:**
   Advancement and Troublesome Innovations: While mechanical interruptions present difficulties, they likewise present huge venture amazing open doors. Advancements in regions like man-made consciousness, biotechnology, and sustainable power offer roads for financial backers to gain by groundbreaking innovations.
   Fintech and Computerized Change: The monetary innovation (Fintech) upheaval has set out open doors in advanced banking, online installment

frameworks, and blockchain innovations. Financial backers can investigate Fintech developments that upgrade productivity and offer imaginative monetary types of assistance.

2. **Reasonable and Effect Money management:**
   ESG Ventures: The developing accentuation on ecological, social, and administration (ESG) factors opens up open doors for practical speculations. Financial backers can adjust their portfolios to organizations that focus on dependable strategic policies and add to positive cultural and natural results.
   Environmentally friendly power and Clean Advances: With the worldwide spotlight on fighting environmental change, interests in sustainable power and clean advances are acquiring noticeable quality. Financial backers can take part in the progress to a more manageable energy scene.

3. **Developing Business sectors:**
   Undiscovered Development Potential: Developing business sectors offer significant development potential because of elements, for example, rising working class populaces, expanded purchaser spending, and continuous monetary turn of events. Financial backers can expand their portfolios by investigating open doors in these business sectors.
   Framework Advancement: Foundation projects in developing business sectors, including transportation, energy, and broadcast communications, give venture possibilities. These tasks add to financial turn of events and can offer alluring returns for financial backers.

4. **Medical care and Biotechnology:**
   Clinical Development: Advances in medical services and biotechnology present venture open doors. Forward leaps in clinical exploration, drugs, and medical services advances can prompt significant returns for financial backers.
   Maturing Populace Patterns: Segment shifts, especially the maturing worldwide populace, set out open doors in areas like medical care, senior living, and clinical benefits. Financial backers can benefit from the developing interest for items and administrations custom fitted to more established socioeconomics.

5. **Strong Enterprises:**

Fundamental Administrations: Putting resources into fundamental administrations and ventures that show strength during monetary slumps can give steadiness to speculation portfolios. Areas like utilities, medical services, and fundamental customer products frequently exhibit steady interest.

Innovation Empowered Administrations: Enterprises that influence innovation to offer fundamental types of assistance, for example, distant coordinated effort devices, online schooling, and telemedicine, have exhibited versatility and development potential, especially with regards to worldwide disturbances.

III. **Techniques for Financial backers:**

1. **Enhancement:**
   Resource Portion: Expansion across resource classes, topographies, and areas mitigates risk. An even portfolio can give dependability during market variances and catch open doors in various economic situations.
   Elective Speculations: Investigating elective ventures, like confidential value, land, and mutual funds, can improve portfolio enhancement and proposition returns less related with conventional resource classes.
2. **Risk The executives:**
   Risk Evaluation: It is urgent to Lead intensive gamble appraisals. Financial backers need to distinguish and dissect potential dangers related with international occasions, monetary circumstances, and industry-explicit variables to pursue informed venture choices.
   Supporting Methodologies: Carrying out supporting techniques, like choices, prospects, and different subordinates, can assist financial backers with shielding their portfolios from disadvantage risk. Supporting can be especially significant during times of elevated vulnerability.
3. **Research and A reasonable level of investment:**
   Inside and out Examination: Intensive exploration and a reasonable level of effort are key to effective contributing. Breaking down fiscal reports, industry patterns, and the cutthroat scene gives financial backers significant experiences for navigation.
   Natural and Social Effect: For maintainable and influence financial backers, surveying the ecological and social effect of ventures is fundamental. This includes grasping an organization's obligation to ESG standards and assessing its commitments to positive cultural and ecological results.
4. **Long haul Point of view:**
   Persistence and Discipline: Taking on a drawn out venture point of view requires tolerance and discipline. Financial backers who center around the essentials of their ventures and oppose momentary market vacillations are many times better situated to climate unpredictability.
   Key Preparation: Fostering an essential money growth strategy that lines up with long haul monetary objectives assists financial backers with remaining on track. Occasional surveys and acclimations to the arrangement can oblige changing economic situations and individual monetary goals.
5. **Nonstop Learning:**

   Remain Informed: The venture scene is dynamic, and remaining informed about market patterns, monetary pointers, and worldwide occasions is pivotal. Ceaseless learning empowers financial backers to adjust to changing conditions and pursue informed choices.

Versatility: Markets are dependent upon future developments, and flexibility is a critical property for fruitful financial backers. Being available to new venture open doors, changing systems in light of economic situations, and gaining from the two victories and disappointments add to long haul achievement.

Investment Strategies in FTT

9.1 Investment Strategies in FTT

The coming of Monetary Exchange Duty (FTT) presents a change in outlook in the worldwide monetary scene, impacting the way of behaving of financial backers and reshaping conventional speculation methodologies. FTT, described by a little duty on different monetary exchanges, means to create income for legislatures and check exorbitant hypothesis.

In exploring this new period, financial backers are constrained to reevaluate their methodologies, taking into account the ramifications, difficulties, and open doors inborn in a monetary environment subject to exchange charges.

Long haul Effective financial planning:

A vital technique in the period of FTT is the accentuation on long haul effective money management. With the expense intended to deter transient hypothesis, financial backers are finding charm in a purchase and-hold approach. By zeroing in on resources with vigorous basics and development possible over a lengthy period, financial backers can relieve the effect of FTT on exchange recurrence. This essential shift lines up with the expense's aims as well as offers the advantage of lower exchanging costs over the long run.

Portfolio Broadening:

In light of FTT, portfolio enhancement accepts uplifted importance as financial backers try to spread risk across different resource classes, geographic areas, and businesses. The reasoning behind this technique lies in limiting the taxation rate on unambiguous exchanges by conveying ventures in a calculated way. An enhanced portfolio goes about as a gamble the executives instrument, permitting financial backers to explore the difficulties presented by FTT while streamlining returns.

Center around Profit Yielding Stocks:

A nuanced procedure includes an elevated spotlight on profit yielding stocks. These stocks become an alluring choice as they offer a kind of revenue for financial backers, and profits are ordinarily excluded from FTT. Lining up with a duty effective venture approach, financial backers might incline toward stocks with a background marked by reliable profits, planning to produce returns while moderating openness to the expense ramifications of regular exchanges.

Using Expense Advantaged Records:

Financial backers are investigating the benefits of assessment advantaged records to enhance their profits in the period of FTT. Retirement or investment accounts, offering tax breaks on commitments and profit, become important instruments for safeguarding a part of speculations from FTT. This essential move lines up with more extensive duty arranging targets, underlining the significance of after-government forms in a burdened monetary climate.

Algorithmic Exchanging Changes:

For financial backers utilizing algorithmic exchanging systems, changes are basic to oblige the subtleties of FTT. High-recurrence exchanging (HFT) systems, portrayed by a high volume of exchanges, may see decreased benefit because of the expense influence. Financial backers utilizing algorithmic methodologies should adjust their techniques to improve execution in a burdened climate, possibly refining calculations to decrease exchanging recurrence or investigating elective exchanging strategies.

Risk The executives Methodologies:

FTT presents an extra layer of cost to exchanges, making strong gamble the board procedures central for financial backers. In this unique situation, complete gamble evaluations, situation examinations, and supporting methodologies become the overwhelming focus. Financial backers should explore the effect of FTT by carrying out measures that defend their portfolios against unanticipated market developments, subsequently guaranteeing the protection of portfolio esteem.

Difficulties and Contemplations:

While these venture methodologies offer roads to explore the difficulties presented by FTT, certain contemplations and difficulties merit consideration. One critical test is the expected effect on market liquidity. FTT has the ability to decrease liquidity, prompting more extensive bid-ask spreads and expected hardships in executing exchanges. To address this test, financial backers need to painstakingly assess the liquidity ramifications of FTT and investigate imaginative arrangements, for example, block exchanging or elective liquidity suppliers.

One more basic thought is the appraisal of exchange costs. FTT straightforwardly expands these expenses, inciting financial backers to lead an exhaustive money saving advantage examination. Finding some kind of harmony between expected returns and the extra expenses related with FTT is fundamental, directing financial backers toward methodologies that line up with their gamble bring inclinations back.

Furthermore, versatility to administrative changes arises as an essential thought. Financial backers should stay adaptable and versatile despite advancing administrative scenes. Administrative changes might affect the possibility and viability of specific systems, requiring continuous carefulness and an eagerness to change speculation approaches because of moving administrative structures.

9.2 Potential Returns and Risks

Contributing is a dynamic and diverse movement that requires a cautious harmony between possible returns and dangers. Whether you are a carefully prepared financial backer or a beginner hoping to enter the monetary business sectors, understanding the interaction between these two basic components is fundamental for going with informed choices. In this thorough investigation, we will dig into the idea of possible returns and dangers, analyzing their importance, factors impacting them, and methodologies to upgrade the sensitive balance among remuneration and risk.

1. **The Meaning of Expected Returns**

   Potential returns address the increases a financial backer expects from a speculation over a predefined period. These profits can take different structures, including capital appreciation, profits, interest, or a blend of these. The charm of potential returns lies in the valuable chance to develop riches and accomplish monetary objectives. To fathom the meaning of possible returns, it's pivotal to investigate the variables that add to their fluctuation.

   Economic situations:

   Market elements assume a significant part in deciding possible returns. Buyer markets, described by rising costs and positive financial backer feeling, frequently yield better yields. On the other hand, bear markets, set apart by falling costs and negativity, can restrict likely returns. Financial backers need to adjust their techniques to the common economic situations to expand returns.

   Monetary Markers:

   Monetary markers, for example, Gross domestic product development, expansion rates, and joblessness figures, impact possible returns. A hearty economy by and large encourages better yields, while financial slumps might present difficulties. Financial backers should remain receptive to macroeconomic variables to precisely evaluate expected returns.

   Industry and Area Patterns:

   Various businesses and areas display particular development examples and hazard profiles. Putting resources into areas with solid development potential can upgrade possible returns, yet it likewise opens financial backers to area explicit dangers. A broadened portfolio traversing different businesses mitigates these dangers.

   Organization Execution:

   The monetary wellbeing and execution of individual organizations altogether influence expected returns. Intensive examination into an organization's basics, including profit, income, and market position, is critical for pursuing informed speculation choices.

2. **The Idea of Dangers in Venture**

   While potential returns are tempting, they come connected at the hip with gambles. Takes a chance in the venture scene are the vulnerabilities and potential disadvantages that financial backers face. Understanding the idea of these dangers is fundamental for creating a versatile speculation methodology.

   Market Hazard:

   Market risk, otherwise called orderly gamble, comes from expansive financial and market factors. It incorporates occasions like market declines, monetary downturns, and international disturbance. Enhancement across resource classes and geographic districts can assist with relieving market risk.

Organization Explicit Gamble:
Organization explicit or unsystematic gamble is attached to individual organizations. Factors like unfortunate administration choices, item disappointments, or legitimate issues can influence a particular organization's presentation. Enhancing across various organizations inside a portfolio helps offset organization explicit gamble.

Financing cost Hazard:
Financing cost developments impact the worth of fixed-pay protections. At the point when financing costs rise, bond costs will more often than not fall, prompting possible misfortunes for bond financial backers. Understanding loan fee risk is urgent for those with a critical designation to fixed-pay resources.

Liquidity Chance:
Liquidity risk emerges when it is trying to trade a venture without influencing its cost. Interests in less fluid resources, like specific stocks or confidential value, may confront liquidity challenges. Financial backers ought to consider their liquidity needs and the liquidity of their speculations.

3. **Methodologies for Adjusting Returns and Dangers**

The craft of effective putting lies in finding some kind of harmony between expected returns and dangers. A few techniques can assist financial backers with exploring this complicated territory:

Broadening:
Broadening a portfolio across various resource classes, enterprises, and geographic locales is a reliable procedure for overseeing risk. A very much enhanced portfolio is less powerless against the unfriendly effect of a solitary venture or market fragment.

Risk Resilience Evaluation:
Understanding one's gamble resilience is essential. Financial backers should survey their capacity and eagerness to endure changes in the worth of their ventures. This evaluation directs the choice of speculations lined up with individual gamble profiles.

Exhaustive Exploration:
Directing intensive exploration prior to pursuing venture choices is vital. Whether putting resources into individual stocks, shared reserves, or other monetary instruments, a profound comprehension of the fundamental resources is fundamental for relieving gambles and expanding likely returns.

Standard Observing and Rebalancing:
Monetary business sectors are dynamic, and financial circumstances develop. Consistently checking the exhibition of speculations and rebalancing the portfolio in light of changing economic situations keeps up with the ideal gamble bring profile back.

Long haul Point of view:

Embracing a drawn out venture point of view permits financial backers to brave transient market variances. Market instability is a characteristic piece of effective financial planning, and an emphasis on long haul objectives can assist financial backers with remaining restrained and abstain from pursuing imprudent choices during market slumps.

Risk The board Apparatuses:

Using risk the executives instruments, for example, stop-misfortune orders and choices, can assist with alleviating drawback gambles. These devices give a degree of security via consequently setting off activities when certain predefined conditions are met.

Proficient Direction:

Looking for exhortation from monetary experts, like monetary counselors or venture directors, can be important. Experts can give custom-made direction in light of individual monetary objectives, risk resistance, and economic situations.

9.3 Diversification in a Tokenized Economy

In the quickly developing scene of money and venture, the coming of blockchain innovation has introduced another period with the ascent of tokenization. Tokenization alludes to the method involved with switching freedoms over completely to a resource into a computerized token on a blockchain. This progressive improvement has significant ramifications for the idea of expansion, empowering financial backers to explore the intricacies of the cutting edge monetary environment. In this broad investigation, we dig into the elements of expansion in a tokenized economy, looking at the advantages, difficulties, and future ramifications of this extraordinary shift.

1. **Figuring out Tokenization and Its Effect on Broadening**

   Tokenization Basics:

   At its center, tokenization includes addressing proprietorship or privileges to a resource as a computerized token on a blockchain. This can apply to a wide cluster of resources, including land, stocks, craftsmanship, and, surprisingly, protected innovation. Every token is remarkable, recognizable, and ordinarily distinct, giving uncommon granularity in possession.

   Separating Customary Obstructions:

   Customary venture markets have for some time been described by hindrances to passage, absence of liquidity, and lumbering cycles. Tokenization kills a large number of these obstructions by working with partial proprietorship, empowering financial backers to trade more modest segments of high-esteem resources. This democratization of access advances inclusivity and expands the financial backer base.

   Upgraded Liquidity:

   Liquidity, a critical calculate speculation achievement, gets a huge lift through tokenization. By empowering fragmentary possession and making an optional market for exchanging tokens, financial backers gain the capacity to proficiently sell their property more. This newly discovered liquidity not just decreases the time and cost related with trading resources yet in addition improves portfolio adaptability.

Worldwide Availability:
Tokenization rises above geological limits, giving financial backers phenomenal admittance to a worldwide commercial center. Computerized tokens can be exchanged consistently on blockchain-based stages, killing the requirement for middle people and smoothing out cross-line exchanges. This worldwide openness improves expansion amazing open doors by permitting financial backers to investigate resources from various districts and markets.

2. **Advantages of Expansion in a Tokenized Economy**
Resource Assortment Past Customary Classes:
Expansion generally includes spreading speculations across various resource classes, like stocks, bonds, and land. In a tokenized economy, the extent of enhancement grows past conventional limits. Financial backers can differentiate across an expansive range of tokenized resources, including intriguing workmanship, funding tasks, and even income sharing arrangements attached to licensed innovation.

Partial Possession and Openness:
Tokenization empowers fragmentary proprietorship, permitting financial backers to get to high-esteem resources with restricted capital. This fractionalization not just upgrades enhancement by expanding the scope of investable resources yet in addition mitigates takes a chance by spreading openness across a bigger number of property.

Diminished Counterparty Chance:
Customary ventures frequently include different middle people, presenting counterparty risk. In a tokenized economy, brilliant agreements on blockchain networks mechanize and uphold legally binding arrangements, decreasing dependence on mediators. This lessens counterparty risk, making the venture cycle more straightforward, effective, and secure.

all day, every day Market Availability:
The decentralized idea of blockchain networks guarantees nonstop market availability. Customary monetary business sectors are dependent upon explicit working hours and time regions. In a tokenized economy, financial backers can exchange computerized resources nonstop, giving open doors to enhancement and chance administration whenever.

Improved Portfolio Straightforwardness:
Blockchain innovation, the underpinning of tokenization, carries unmatched straightforwardness to exchanges. Each exchange is recorded on a changeless record, permitting financial backers to follow the proprietorship history of

tokens. This straightforwardness encourages trust as well as engages financial backers to pursue more educated choices while enhancing their portfolios.

3. **Difficulties and Contemplations in Tokenized Expansion**

   Administrative Vulnerability:

   The administrative scene encompassing tokenized resources is as yet advancing. Various wards have differed ways to deal with tokenization, making a level of vulnerability for financial backers.

   Understanding and exploring the administrative climate is essential to guarantee consistence and moderate administrative dangers related with tokenized expansion.

   Market Development and Instability:

   While tokenization presents invigorating potential outcomes, the market is still moderately youthful and can be inclined to higher instability. Financial backers should cautiously evaluate the development of tokenized showcases and be ready for potential cost changes. As the market develops, instability might diminish, giving a more steady climate to differentiated portfolios.

   Innovation Dangers:

   The dependence on blockchain innovation presents its own arrangement of dangers. Issues like brilliant agreement weaknesses, network security, and versatility moves should be tended to. Financial backers should remain informed about innovative turns of events, draw in with secure stages, and consider the vigor of the basic blockchain foundation.

   Absence of Normalization:

   The tokenized economy needs normalized works on, prompting various symbolic guidelines and stages. This absence of consistency presents difficulties for financial backers looking to enhance across changed resources and stages. Endeavors to lay out industry guidelines and interoperability are fundamental for encouraging a more firm and open tokenized biological system.

4. **Future Patterns and Suggestions**

   Development of Tokenized Resources:

   The extent of tokenization is supposed to grow past customary resource classes. As the innovation develops and administrative structures become more characterized, we can expect the tokenization of a more extensive scope of resources, including licensed innovation, carbon credits, and that's only the tip of the iceberg. This extension will additionally upgrade enhancement amazing open doors.

   Advancement of Safety Token Contributions (STOs):

   Security Token Contributions, which address possession in genuine resources, are probably going to acquire conspicuousness. STOs give a managed and consistent method for giving tokenized protections. This advancement is supposed to bring expanded institutional cooperation and administrative lucidity to the tokenized economy, reinforcing financial backer certainty.

Incorporation of Decentralized Money (DeFi):

The convergence of tokenization and decentralized finance (DeFi) is a promising outskirts. DeFi stages influence blockchain innovation to reproduce customary monetary administrations like loaning, acquiring, and exchanging without conventional delegates. The reconciliation of DeFi with tokenized resources could reclassify how financial backers approach enhancement and hazard the executives.

Interoperability and Normalization:

Endeavors to lay out interoperability principles and smooth out tokenization processes are in progress. As the business develops, we can expect expanded joint effort among blockchain projects and the advancement of broad guidelines. This will improve on the broadening system for financial backers and add to the general development of the tokenized economy.

Printed in the USA
CPSIA information can be obtained
at www.ICGtesting.com
LVHW010622310524
781705LV00001B/34